Super easy DIABETIC AIR FRYER Cookbook for Beginners

QUICK, TASTY, AND DIABETES-FRIENDLY RECIPES FOR EVERY MEAL. INCLUDES A 28-DAY PLAN

Gertraud Kron

TABLE OF CONTENT

Chapter 1: Introduction

Welcome to Diabetic Air Fryer Cooking

Welcome to "Diabetic Air Fryer Cookbook for Beginners"! Whether you've just been diagnosed with diabetes, are looking to improve your dietary habits, or simply want to explore healthier cooking methods, this book is designed to be your ultimate guide. We understand that managing diabetes can be challenging, and finding recipes that are both delicious and suitable for your dietary needs may seem daunting. That's why we've created this comprehensive resource to help you navigate the world of diabetes-friendly cooking with the convenience of an air fryer.

The Benefits of Air Fryer Cooking

Air fryers have revolutionized the way we cook, offering a healthier alternative to traditional frying methods. Here are some key benefits of using an air fryer, especially for those managing diabetes:

- **Reduced Oil Consumption**: Air fryers use hot air circulation to cook food, requiring significantly less oil compared to traditional frying. This reduction in oil can help lower your intake of unhealthy fats, which is crucial for managing blood sugar levels and overall heart health.
- **Lower Calorie Meals**: By using less oil, air-fried foods tend to be lower in calories, helping you maintain a healthy weight, which is essential for diabetes management.
- **Retained Nutrients**: Air fryers cook food quickly, preserving more nutrients compared to some other cooking methods. This ensures that your meals are not only healthy but also nutritious.

- **Convenience and Speed**: Air fryers are incredibly user-friendly and can significantly reduce cooking times. This is perfect for busy individuals who need to prepare quick, healthy meals without spending hours in the kitchen.
- **Versatility**: Air fryers can be used for a wide range of cooking tasks, from frying and roasting to baking and grilling. This versatility allows you to prepare a variety of diabetes-friendly dishes that are both delicious and satisfying.

How This Book Will Help You Manage Diabetes

This book is not just a collection of recipes; it's a comprehensive guide to understanding and managing diabetes through diet and lifestyle. Here's what you can expect to gain from "Diabetic Air Fryer Cookbook for Beginners":

1. **Expert Nutritional Guidance**: Each recipe in this book has been carefully crafted to ensure it meets the nutritional requirements for managing diabetes. You'll find detailed nutritional information for every dish, making it easy to track your intake of carbs, fats, and proteins.

2. **Easy-to-Follow Recipes**: We've designed our recipes with beginners in mind. Each recipe includes clear, step-by-step instructions, cooking times, and tips to help you achieve perfect results every time.

3. **Practical Cooking Tips**: Learn the basics of using an air fryer, from selecting the right model to understanding its various functions. Our practical tips will help you maximize the benefits of your air fryer and make cooking a breeze.

4. **Delicious and Varied Meals**: Our recipes cover a wide range of meals, from breakfast and snacks to main courses and desserts. You'll never get bored with our diverse selection of dishes, ensuring that you enjoy your meals while managing your diabetes.

5. **Meal Planning and Lifestyle Advice**: In addition to recipes, we provide guidance on meal planning, portion control, and maintaining a balanced diet. You'll also find tips on incorporating physical activity, managing stress, and monitoring your blood sugar levels.

Structure of the Book

"Diabetic Air Fryer Cookbook for Beginners" is divided into several sections to provide you with a comprehensive understanding of diabetic cooking with an air fryer:

- **Part 1: Getting Started**: This section introduces you to the basics of diabetes management and air fryer cooking. You'll learn about the types of air fryers, essential accessories, and tips for setting up and maintaining your air fryer.
- **Part 2: Mastering Air Fryer Cooking**: Here, we delve into air fryer techniques, including preheating, cooking times, and achieving the perfect crispiness. You'll also learn how to adapt traditional recipes for the air fryer.

- **Part 3: Recipes**: This section is packed with a wide range of delicious, diabetes-friendly recipes, from breakfast delights and snacks to main courses, vegetarian options, sides, and healthy desserts.
- **Part 4: Meal Planning and Beyond**: Learn how to plan balanced meals, calculate nutritional information, and incorporate a healthy lifestyle into your daily routine.
- **Part 5: Resources**: Find answers to frequently asked questions, a glossary of cooking and nutritional terms, conversion charts, and recommended readings.

Encouragement and Support

Embarking on a journey to manage diabetes can be challenging, but you are not alone. This book is here to support and guide you every step of the way. Remember, managing diabetes is not about deprivation but about making informed choices that support your health and well-being.

As you explore the recipes and tips in this book, we encourage you to experiment, have fun, and enjoy the process of discovering new, healthy dishes that you and your loved ones will love. Together, we can make diabetes-friendly cooking a delightful and rewarding experience.

Welcome to a healthier, happier way of cooking and eating with "Diabetic Air Fryer Cookbook for Beginners"!

Chapter 2: What is "Diabetic Air Fryer Cookbook for Beginners"?

Introduction to "Diabetic Air Fryer Cookbook for Beginners"

"Diabetic Air Fryer Cookbook for Beginners" is a comprehensive guide designed to help individuals manage diabetes through healthy, delicious, and easy-to-prepare meals using an air fryer. This book is not just a collection of recipes; it is a complete resource that provides valuable information, practical tips, and step-by-step instructions to make diabetes-friendly cooking enjoyable and accessible for everyone, especially beginners.

Purpose and Goals

The primary goal of this book is to empower you with the knowledge and skills needed to create nutritious and tasty meals that support diabetes management. By leveraging the convenience and versatility of an air fryer, this book aims to:

- **Simplify Healthy Cooking**: Make it easier for you to prepare healthy meals without spending hours in the kitchen.

- **Enhance Your Culinary Skills**: Provide you with the confidence to use your air fryer effectively and adapt traditional recipes to fit your dietary needs.
- **Support Diabetes Management**: Offer recipes and nutritional guidance that help you maintain stable blood sugar levels and improve your overall health.
- **Promote Enjoyment of Food**: Show that eating healthily can be delicious and varied, dispelling the myth that a diabetes-friendly diet is bland or boring.

Key Features of the Book

1. **Detailed Nutritional Information**: Each recipe includes comprehensive nutritional breakdowns, including calories, carbohydrates, fats, proteins, fiber, and sugar content. This information helps you make informed choices about your meals and manage your carbohydrate intake effectively.

2. **Beginner-Friendly Instructions**: The recipes are designed with beginners in mind, featuring clear, step-by-step instructions that are easy to follow. You don't need to be an experienced cook to create these dishes successfully.

3. **Wide Range of Recipes**: The book covers a variety of meal categories, including breakfasts, snacks, main courses, vegetarian options, sides, and desserts. This ensures that you have a diverse selection of meals to choose from, keeping your diet interesting and satisfying.

4. **Practical Tips and Tricks**: Alongside the recipes, you'll find practical advice on using your air fryer, such as cooking times, temperature settings, and tips for achieving the best results. This guidance helps you make the most of your air fryer and cook like a pro.

5. **Meal Planning Guidance**: Beyond individual recipes, the book offers advice on planning balanced meals, grocery shopping, and maintaining a healthy lifestyle. This holistic approach ensures that you have all the tools you need to manage your diabetes effectively.

Understanding Diabetes and Diet

To fully appreciate the benefits of this book, it's essential to understand the relationship between diabetes and diet. Diabetes is a chronic condition that affects how your body processes glucose, leading to elevated blood sugar levels. Managing diabetes involves balancing medication, physical activity, and, crucially, diet.

Key Dietary Considerations for Diabetes Management:

- **Carbohydrate Control**: Monitoring carbohydrate intake is vital, as carbohydrates have the most significant impact on blood sugar levels. The recipes in this book are designed to help you control your carbohydrate intake while still enjoying delicious meals.
- **Healthy Fats**: Incorporating healthy fats, such as those found in olive oil, nuts, and avocados, can help manage cholesterol levels and reduce the risk of heart disease, which is crucial for individuals with diabetes.

- **Fiber-Rich Foods**: High-fiber foods can help regulate blood sugar levels and improve digestion. The recipes in this book emphasize the inclusion of fiber-rich vegetables, whole grains, and legumes.
- **Protein Balance**: Including lean protein sources in your diet helps with satiety and blood sugar control. This book offers a variety of protein-rich recipes, including both animal and plant-based options.

The Role of the Air Fryer

The air fryer is a revolutionary kitchen appliance that uses hot air circulation to cook food, producing a crispy texture similar to frying but with significantly less oil. This makes it an ideal tool for preparing healthy, diabetes-friendly meals.

Benefits of Using an Air Fryer:

- **Healthier Cooking**: By using minimal oil, air fryers reduce the fat and calorie content of your meals, helping you maintain a healthy weight and manage diabetes more effectively.
- **Versatility**: Air fryers can roast, bake, grill, and fry, allowing you to prepare a wide range of dishes. This versatility is reflected in the diverse recipes provided in this book.
- **Convenience**: Air fryers cook food quickly and are easy to use, making healthy cooking more accessible for busy individuals.
- **Flavor and Texture**: Air fryers produce delicious, crispy results that are often superior to traditional cooking methods, ensuring that healthy meals are enjoyable and satisfying.

What You Will Learn

By reading "Diabetic Air Fryer Cookbook for Beginners," you will:

- **Understand Diabetes-Friendly Ingredients**: Learn about the best ingredients to use in your cooking and how they can help manage your diabetes.
- **Master Air Fryer Techniques**: Gain confidence in using your air fryer through practical tips and detailed instructions.
- **Create Nutritious and Delicious Meals**: Access a variety of recipes that are both healthy and flavorful, making it easier to stick to a diabetes-friendly diet.
- **Plan Balanced Meals**: Get guidance on meal planning and portion control, helping you maintain a balanced diet that supports your health goals.

Conclusion

"Diabetic Air Fryer Cookbook for Beginners" is more than just a cookbook; it's a comprehensive guide to living well with diabetes. By combining the latest nutritional insights with the convenience of air fryer cooking, this book provides you with the tools and knowledge you need to take control of your health and enjoy delicious meals every day. Whether you're new to diabetes management or looking to expand your culinary skills, this book is your essential companion on the journey to healthier living. Welcome to a new world of tasty, diabetes-friendly cooking!

Chapter 3: Introduction: Causes and Types of Diabetes

Understanding Diabetes

Diabetes is a chronic medical condition characterized by high levels of glucose (sugar) in the blood. It occurs when the body either does not produce enough insulin or cannot effectively use the insulin it produces. Insulin is a hormone produced by the pancreas that helps glucose enter the cells of the body, where it is used for energy. When glucose builds up in the blood instead of being used by cells, it can lead to various health problems.

Causes of Diabetes

The exact cause of diabetes varies depending on the type of diabetes. However, common factors contributing to the development of diabetes include genetic, environmental, and lifestyle factors.

1. **Genetic Factors**: Family history plays a significant role in the likelihood of developing diabetes. If one or both parents have diabetes, the risk of developing the condition increases.
2. **Autoimmune Destruction**: In type 1 diabetes, the immune system mistakenly attacks and destroys insulin-producing beta cells in the pancreas. This autoimmune response is often triggered by genetic factors and possibly environmental factors such as viruses.
3. **Insulin Resistance**: In type 2 diabetes, the body's cells become resistant to the effects of insulin. As a result, the pancreas produces more insulin to try to compensate, but over time it cannot keep up, leading to elevated blood sugar levels.
4. **Obesity and Physical Inactivity**: Excess body fat, particularly around the abdomen, is a major risk factor for type 2 diabetes. Physical inactivity also contributes to insulin resistance and the development of diabetes.
5. **Hormonal Changes**: Certain conditions, such as polycystic ovary syndrome (PCOS), and hormonal changes during pregnancy can increase the risk of developing diabetes.
6. **Poor Diet**: Diets high in refined sugars, unhealthy fats, and low in fiber can contribute to obesity and insulin resistance, increasing the risk of type 2 diabetes.

Types of Diabetes

There are several types of diabetes, each with different causes and management strategies. The most common types are type 1, type 2, and gestational diabetes.

Type 1 Diabetes

- **Description**: Type 1 diabetes, previously known as juvenile diabetes or insulin-dependent diabetes, is an autoimmune condition where the body's immune system attacks the insulin-producing beta cells in the pancreas. This leads to little or no insulin production.

- **Causes**: The exact cause is unknown, but it is believed to involve a combination of genetic susceptibility and environmental factors, such as viral infections.
- **Management**: People with type 1 diabetes require lifelong insulin therapy to manage blood sugar levels. This includes multiple daily injections or the use of an insulin pump. Regular monitoring of blood glucose levels, a balanced diet, and physical activity are also crucial for managing type 1 diabetes.

Type 2 Diabetes

- **Description**: Type 2 diabetes, formerly known as adult-onset or non-insulin-dependent diabetes, is the most common form of diabetes. It occurs when the body becomes resistant to insulin or when the pancreas fails to produce enough insulin.
- **Causes**: Type 2 diabetes is primarily associated with genetic factors, obesity, physical inactivity, and poor diet. It is more common in adults but is increasingly seen in younger individuals due to rising obesity rates.
- **Management**: Management includes lifestyle changes such as adopting a healthy diet, increasing physical activity, and maintaining a healthy weight. Medications and insulin therapy may be required to control blood sugar levels. Monitoring blood glucose levels regularly is also essential.

Gestational Diabetes

- **Description**: Gestational diabetes develops during pregnancy and usually disappears after giving birth. However, it increases the risk of developing type 2 diabetes later in life.
- **Causes**: Hormonal changes during pregnancy can make the body less responsive to insulin. Risk factors include being overweight, having a family history of diabetes, and previous gestational diabetes.
- **Management**: Management involves a healthy diet, regular physical activity, and monitoring blood sugar levels. In some cases, insulin or other medications may be needed.

Other Types of Diabetes

- **Monogenic Diabetes**: This rare form of diabetes results from a mutation in a single gene. It often appears in adolescence or early adulthood and is managed similarly to other types of diabetes.
- **Secondary Diabetes**: This type of diabetes results from other medical conditions or medications that affect insulin production or function, such as pancreatitis or steroid use.

The Role of Diet in Managing Diabetes

Diet plays a crucial role in managing all types of diabetes. Proper nutrition helps control blood sugar levels, maintain a healthy weight, and reduce the risk of complications. Key dietary principles include:

- **Carbohydrate Management**: Monitoring and managing carbohydrate intake is essential for controlling blood sugar levels. Choose complex carbohydrates with a low glycemic index, such as whole grains, legumes, and non-starchy vegetables.

- **Healthy Fats**: Incorporate healthy fats from sources like olive oil, nuts, seeds, and avocados. Limit saturated and trans fats to improve heart health.
- **Lean Proteins**: Include lean protein sources such as poultry, fish, beans, and tofu to help with satiety and muscle maintenance.
- **Fiber-Rich Foods**: High-fiber foods, including fruits, vegetables, and whole grains, help regulate blood sugar levels and improve digestive health.
- **Portion Control**: Eating appropriate portion sizes helps manage calorie intake and maintain a healthy weight.
- **Regular Meals**: Consistent meal times help stabilize blood sugar levels. Avoid skipping meals to prevent blood sugar spikes and drops.

How "Diabetic Air Fryer Cookbook for Beginners" Can Help

This book is designed to support you in managing diabetes through diet and lifestyle changes. By leveraging the convenience of an air fryer, you can prepare healthy, diabetes-friendly meals with ease. Here's how this book can help:

1. **Simplified Cooking**: Learn how to use your air fryer to create delicious, healthy meals with minimal effort.
2. **Nutritional Guidance**: Gain insights into how different foods affect blood sugar levels and how to balance your meals.
3. **Diverse Recipes**: Access a variety of recipes that cater to different tastes and dietary needs, ensuring you never get bored with your diet.
4. **Practical Tips**: Benefit from practical tips on managing diabetes through diet, including portion control and meal planning.
5. **Healthy Lifestyle**: Discover strategies for incorporating physical activity, managing stress, and maintaining overall health.

By understanding the causes and types of diabetes and how to manage it through diet and lifestyle, you can take control of your health and enjoy delicious, nutritious meals every day. "Diabetic Air Fryer Cookbook for Beginners" is your comprehensive guide to achieving these goals and living well with diabetes.

Chapter 4: Benefits of the "Diabetic Air Fryer Cookbook for Beginners"

Adopting a healthier lifestyle and managing diabetes can feel overwhelming, especially when it comes to cooking. "Diabetic Air Fryer Cookbook for Beginners" is designed to simplify this journey, providing you with practical tools and delicious recipes that support your health goals. This chapter highlights the numerous benefits you'll gain from this cookbook, emphasizing how it can transform your approach to eating and diabetes management.

Health Benefits

1. **Improved Blood Sugar Control**
   - **Balanced Nutritional Profiles**: Each recipe in this cookbook is carefully crafted to ensure a balanced intake of carbohydrates, proteins, and fats, which are crucial for maintaining stable blood sugar levels.
   - **Low Glycemic Ingredients**: The recipes emphasize the use of low glycemic index (GI) foods, which help prevent blood sugar spikes and crashes, contributing to better diabetes management.

2. **Weight Management**
   o **Reduced Calorie Intake**: Air frying significantly reduces the need for oil, cutting down on unnecessary calories and unhealthy fats. This aids in weight management, which is essential for controlling diabetes.
   o **Portion Control**: The cookbook provides clear serving sizes and portion control guidelines, helping you avoid overeating and maintain a healthy weight.

3. **Enhanced Heart Health**
   o **Healthy Fats**: Recipes focus on incorporating healthy fats from sources like olive oil, nuts, and avocados, while minimizing saturated and trans fats. This helps improve cholesterol levels and reduce the risk of heart disease.
   o **Reduced Sodium**: Many recipes offer alternatives to high-sodium ingredients, promoting better blood pressure control and overall cardiovascular health.

4. **Nutrient-Rich Meals**
   o **High Fiber Content**: The inclusion of fiber-rich foods such as vegetables, whole grains, and legumes aids in digestion, helps regulate blood sugar levels, and promotes satiety.
   o **Vital Vitamins and Minerals**: Recipes are designed to include a variety of nutrient-dense ingredients, ensuring you receive essential vitamins and minerals that support overall health.

Practical Benefits

1. **Convenience and Ease of Use**
   o **Time-Saving Recipes**: Air fryers cook food quickly, significantly reducing meal preparation time. This is perfect for busy individuals who need to prepare healthy meals without spending hours in the kitchen.
   o **Beginner-Friendly Instructions**: Each recipe comes with step-by-step instructions, making it easy for beginners to follow and achieve great results.

2. **Versatility in Cooking**
   o **Diverse Recipe Selection**: The cookbook offers a wide range of recipes, from breakfast to dinner and snacks to desserts. This ensures you have plenty of options to keep your meals exciting and varied.
   o **Multiple Cooking Methods**: Learn how to use your air fryer for frying, roasting, baking, and grilling, expanding your culinary skills and allowing you to experiment with different cooking techniques.

3. **Consistency and Reliability**

- o **Proven Recipes**: Each recipe has been tested to ensure it delivers consistent and delicious results. This reliability builds your confidence in cooking and encourages you to try new dishes.
- o **Nutritional Accuracy**: Detailed nutritional information for each recipe helps you monitor your intake of carbohydrates, fats, proteins, and other nutrients, supporting precise diabetes management.

Lifestyle Benefits

1. **Enjoyment of Food**
   - o **Flavorful Meals**: Contrary to the misconception that healthy food is bland, this cookbook provides recipes that are both nutritious and bursting with flavor. Enjoy meals that are as tasty as they are good for you.
   - o **Creative Cooking**: Discover new ways to prepare your favorite foods using the air fryer, making healthy eating an enjoyable and creative experience.
2. **Empowerment and Confidence**
   - o **Knowledge and Skills**: Gain a deeper understanding of how to manage diabetes through diet. With this knowledge, you'll feel more empowered to make healthy choices and take control of your health.
   - o **Independence in the Kitchen**: The easy-to-follow recipes and practical tips give you the confidence to cook independently, regardless of your prior experience.
3. **Community and Support**
   - o **Shared Experiences**: By trying out these recipes and sharing them with family and friends, you can create a supportive environment that encourages healthy eating habits.
   - o **Inspiration and Motivation**: Reading success stories and tips from others who have used the cookbook can inspire you to stay committed to your health journey.

Environmental Benefits

1. **Energy Efficiency**
   - o **Lower Energy Consumption**: Air fryers typically use less energy compared to traditional ovens, making them an environmentally friendly choice for cooking.
   - o **Reduced Cooking Times**: Quicker cooking times mean less energy usage, contributing to a smaller carbon footprint.
2. **Waste Reduction**
   - o **Efficient Use of Ingredients**: The recipes in this cookbook are designed to minimize waste by using whole ingredients and offering tips on how to repurpose leftovers.
   - o **Eco-Friendly Practices**: Emphasis on fresh, whole foods and reducing reliance on processed items promotes a more sustainable approach to eating.

Conclusion

"Diabetic Air Fryer Cookbook for Beginners" offers a multitude of benefits that extend beyond just providing recipes. It is a comprehensive guide that supports your health, simplifies your cooking routine, and enhances your overall lifestyle. By integrating the principles and recipes from this book into your daily life, you can achieve better diabetes management, enjoy delicious meals, and lead a healthier, more fulfilling life.

As you continue your journey with this cookbook, remember that making small, consistent changes can lead to significant improvements in your health and well-being. Embrace the convenience, flavor, and health benefits that come with air fryer cooking, and take control of your diabetes with confidence and joy.

Chapter 5: Shopping List: Foods to Eat and Foods to Avoid

Creating a diabetes-friendly kitchen starts with smart shopping. Knowing which foods to include and which to avoid can make meal planning and preparation easier, healthier, and more enjoyable. This chapter provides comprehensive shopping lists, outlining foods that support your diabetes management and those that should be limited or avoided.

Foods to Eat

Focusing on nutrient-dense, low-glycemic foods is key to maintaining stable blood sugar levels. Here is a detailed list of foods to prioritize:

Category	Food Items
Vegetables	**Non-Starchy Vegetables**: Leafy greens (spinach, kale, arugula), Cruciferous vegetables (broccoli, cauliflower, Brussels sprouts), Peppers (bell peppers, jalapeños), Tomatoes, Cucumbers, Zucchini, Green beans, Asparagus, Mushrooms **Starchy Vegetables (in moderation)**: Sweet potatoes, Squash (butternut, acorn), Peas, Corn
Fruits	**Low-Glycemic Fruits**: Berries (strawberries, blueberries, raspberries, blackberries), Apples, Pears, Oranges, Grapefruit, Peaches, Plums, Cherries, Kiwi
Grains and Legumes	**Whole Grains**: Quinoa, Brown rice, Oats (preferably steel-cut or old-fashioned), Barley, Whole wheat (bread, pasta) **Legumes**: Lentils, Chickpeas, Black beans, Kidney beans, Pinto beans
Proteins	**Lean Animal Proteins**: Chicken breast, Turkey, Fish (salmon, mackerel, sardines), Lean cuts of beef and pork, Eggs **Plant-Based Proteins**: Tofu, Tempeh, Edamame, Nuts (almonds, walnuts, cashews) and seeds (chia seeds, flaxseeds, pumpkin seeds)
Dairy and Alternatives	**Low-Fat Dairy**: Greek yogurt (unsweetened), Skim or low-fat milk, Cottage cheese, Cheese (in moderation) **Dairy Alternatives**: Almond milk, Soy milk, Coconut milk (unsweetened), Nutritional yeast
Healthy Fats	**Oils**: Olive oil, Avocado oil, Coconut oil (in moderation) **Other Healthy Fats**: Avocados, Olives, Nut butters (almond butter, peanut butter, without added sugar)
Beverages	**Hydrating Options**: Water, Herbal teas, Black coffee (without sugar)

Foods to Avoid

Certain foods can cause rapid spikes in blood sugar levels or contribute to other health issues related to diabetes. Here's a list of foods to limit or avoid:

Category	Food Items
Sugary Foods and Drinks	**Sugary Beverages**: Sodas, Sweetened teas, Fruit juices (unless specifically recommended in moderation), Energy drinks **Sweets and Desserts**: Candy, Pastries, Cakes and cookies, Ice cream (except low-sugar or sugar-free options)
Refined Carbohydrates	**White and Processed Grains**: White bread, White rice, Regular pasta, Sugary cereals **Snack Foods**: Potato chips, Pretzels, Crackers (unless whole grain)
Unhealthy Fats	**Trans Fats and Hydrogenated Oils**: Margarine, Shortening, Packaged baked goods **High-Saturated Fat Foods**: Fatty cuts of beef and pork, Processed meats (bacon, sausages), Full-fat dairy products (cream, full-fat cheese)
High-Sodium Foods	**Processed and Packaged Foods**: Canned soups (unless low-sodium), Frozen dinners, Fast food **High-Sodium Snacks**: Salted nuts, Salty snack mixes
High-Glycemic Fruits and Vegetables	**High-Glycemic Fruits (in moderation)**: Watermelon, Pineapple, Overripe bananas **High-Glycemic Vegetables**: Potatoes (especially fried or mashed), Parsnips

Sample Shopping List

Here's a sample shopping list to help you get started. Tailor it to your preferences and dietary needs:

Category	Food Items
Vegetables	Spinach, Broccoli, Bell peppers, Tomatoes, Zucchini
Fruits	Blueberries, Apples, Oranges, Peaches
Grains and Legumes	Quinoa, Brown rice, Oats, Lentils
Proteins	Chicken breast, Salmon, Eggs, Tofu
Dairy and Alternatives	Greek yogurt, Almond milk, Cottage cheese
Healthy Fats	Olive oil, Avocados, Almond butter
Beverages	Water, Herbal tea

Breakfast Recipes

1. Spinach and Feta Egg Muffins

☐☐☐Prep time: 10 min | Cook time: 25 min | Servings: 6 muffins

Ingredients:

- 6 eggs
- 1/2 cup chopped fresh spinach
- 1/4 cup crumbled feta cheese
- 1/4 cup finely diced red bell pepper
- Salt and pepper to taste

Instructions:

1. Preheat the oven to 175 degrees Celsius.
2. Beat eggs in a bowl and season with salt and pepper.
3. Add spinach, feta, and red bell pepper and mix well.
4. Grease muffin tins and evenly distribute the egg mixture.
5. Bake for 25 minutes or until muffins are set.
6. Let cool slightly and serve warm.

Nutrition Facts (per muffin): Calories: 100 kcal | Protein: 7 g | Carbs: 2 g | Fat: 7 g | Fiber: 0.5 g | Sugar: 1 g

2. Low-Carb Breakfast Burritos

Prep time: 15 min | Cook time: 10 min | Servings: 4

Ingredients:

- 4 low-carb tortillas
- 4 eggs
- 1/2 cup diced tomatoes
- 1/2 cup diced avocado
- 1/4 cup shredded cheddar cheese
- 1/4 cup diced onions
- 1 tablespoon olive oil
- Salt and pepper to taste

Instructions:

1. Heat olive oil in a pan over medium heat. Add onions and sauté until translucent.
2. Beat eggs in a bowl, season with salt and pepper, then add to the pan. Scramble until cooked through.
3. Warm tortillas in the air fryer at 180 degrees Celsius for 1-2 minutes.
4. Fill each tortilla with scrambled eggs, tomatoes, avocado, and cheddar cheese.
5. Roll up burritos and serve immediately.

Nutrition Facts (per burrito): Calories: 250 kcal | Protein: 12 g | Carbs: 15 g | Fat: 18 g | Fiber: 8 g | Sugar: 2 g

3. Air Fryer Oatmeal Cups

Prep time: 10 min | Cook time: 15 min | Servings: 12

Ingredients:

- 2 cups rolled oats
- 1 cup mashed bananas
- 1/2 cup almond milk
- 1/4 cup honey
- 1 teaspoon vanilla extract
- 1/2 teaspoon cinnamon
- 1/4 teaspoon salt
- 1/4 cup chopped nuts (optional)

Instructions:

1. Preheat air fryer to 160 degrees Celsius.
2. In a large bowl, combine oats, bananas, almond milk, honey, vanilla extract, cinnamon, and salt. Mix well.
3. Fold in chopped nuts if using.
4. Spoon mixture into silicone muffin cups, filling each about 3/4 full.
5. Place cups in the air fryer basket and cook for 15 minutes or until set.
6. Allow to cool before removing from the cups and serving.

Nutrition Facts (per cup): Calories: 120 kcal | Protein: 3 g | Carbs: 22 g | Fat: 2 g | Fiber: 3 g | Sugar: 8 g

4. Greek Yogurt Parfaits

Prep time: 5 min | Cook time: 0 min | Servings: 4

Ingredients:

- 2 cups plain Greek yogurt
- 1 cup mixed berries (strawberries, blueberries, raspberries)
- 1/2 cup granola
- 2 tablespoons honey
- 1 teaspoon vanilla extract

Instructions:

1. In a bowl, mix Greek yogurt with vanilla extract.
2. Layer yogurt, mixed berries, and granola in four serving glasses.
3. Drizzle honey over the top.
4. Serve immediately or refrigerate until ready to eat.

Nutrition Facts (per serving): Calories: 200 kcal | Protein: 12 g | Carbs: 30 g | Fat: 5 g | Fiber: 4 g | Sugar: 20 g

5. Avocado and Egg Toast

Prep time: 5 min | Cook time: 10 min | Servings: 2

Ingredients:

- 2 slices whole grain bread
- 1 ripe avocado
- 2 eggs
- Salt and pepper to taste
- 1/4 teaspoon red pepper flakes (optional)

Instructions:

1. Toast the whole grain bread slices in the air fryer at 180 degrees Celsius for 3-4 minutes.
2. While the bread is toasting, cook the eggs in a pan to your desired doneness.
3. Mash the avocado and spread it evenly on the toasted bread.
4. Place an egg on each slice of toast.
5. Season with salt, pepper, and red pepper flakes if using.
6. Serve immediately.

Nutrition Facts (per serving): Calories: 250 kcal | Protein: 10 g | Carbs: 20 g | Fat: 15 g | Fiber: 7 g | Sugar: 2 g

6. Blueberry Almond Breakfast Bars

Prep time: 10 min | Cook time: 20 min | Servings: 8

Ingredients:

- 1 cup rolled oats
- 1/2 cup almond flour
- 1/4 cup honey
- 1/4 cup unsweetened applesauce
- 1/2 cup fresh blueberries
- 1/4 cup sliced almonds
- 1 teaspoon vanilla extract
- 1/2 teaspoon cinnamon
- 1/4 teaspoon salt

Instructions:

1. Preheat air fryer to 170 degrees Celsius.
2. In a large bowl, mix oats, almond flour, honey, applesauce, vanilla extract, cinnamon, and salt.
3. Fold in blueberries and sliced almonds.
4. Press the mixture into a greased baking dish that fits into your air fryer.
5. Air fry for 20 minutes or until golden brown and set.
6. Allow to cool before slicing into bars and serving.

Nutrition Facts (per bar): Calories: 150 kcal | Protein: 4 g | Carbs: 24 g | Fat: 6 g | Fiber: 4 g | Sugar: 10 g

7. Cinnamon Apple Air Fryer Donuts

Prep time: 15 min | Cook time: 10 min | Servings: 6

Ingredients:

- 1 cup whole wheat flour
- 1/2 cup unsweetened applesauce
- 1/4 cup honey
- 1 egg
- 1 teaspoon baking powder
- 1/2 teaspoon cinnamon
- 1/4 teaspoon nutmeg
- 1/4 teaspoon salt
- 1 apple, peeled and finely chopped

Instructions:

1. Preheat air fryer to 180 degrees Celsius.
2. In a large bowl, mix flour, baking powder, cinnamon, nutmeg, and salt.
3. In another bowl, whisk together applesauce, honey, and egg.
4. Combine wet and dry ingredients, then fold in chopped apple.
5. Spoon batter into greased donut molds.
6. Air fry for 10 minutes or until a toothpick inserted into the donuts comes out clean.
7. Allow to cool slightly before serving.

Nutrition Facts (per donut): Calories: 120 kcal | Protein: 3 g | Carbs: 26 g | Fat: 1 g | Fiber: 3 g | Sugar: 12 g

8. Veggie-Packed Breakfast Hash

Prep time: 10 min | Cook time: 20 min | Servings: 4

Ingredients:

- 2 medium sweet potatoes, peeled and diced
- 1 red bell pepper, diced
- 1 zucchini, diced
- 1 small onion, diced
- 2 tablespoons olive oil
- 1 teaspoon garlic powder
- 1 teaspoon paprika
- Salt and pepper to taste
- 4 eggs

Instructions:

1. Preheat air fryer to 200 degrees Celsius.
2. In a large bowl, toss sweet potatoes, bell pepper, zucchini, and onion with olive oil, garlic powder, paprika, salt, and pepper.
3. Spread the vegetable mixture in the air fryer basket.
4. Cook for 15 minutes, shaking the basket halfway through.
5. In the last 5 minutes, make small wells in the hash and crack an egg into each well.
6. Continue cooking until eggs are set.
7. Serve immediately.

Nutrition Facts (per serving): Calories: 220 kcal | Protein: 8 g | Carbs: 25 g | Fat: 10 g | Fiber: 5 g | Sugar: 7 g

9. Turkey Sausage Patties

Prep time: 10 min | Cook time: 15 min | Servings: 6 patties

Ingredients:

- 1 pound ground turkey
- 1/4 cup finely chopped onion
- 1 garlic clove, minced
- 1 teaspoon sage
- 1/2 teaspoon thyme
- 1/2 teaspoon salt
- 1/4 teaspoon black pepper
- 1/4 teaspoon red pepper flakes (optional)

Instructions:

1. In a large bowl, combine all ingredients and mix well.
2. Form the mixture into 6 patties.
3. Preheat air fryer to 180 degrees Celsius.
4. Place patties in the air fryer basket in a single layer.
5. Cook for 10-15 minutes, flipping halfway through, until the internal temperature reaches 74 degrees Celsius.

6. Serve warm.

Nutrition Facts (per patty): Calories: 120 kcal | Protein: 16 g | Carbs: 1 g | Fat: 6 g | Fiber: 0 g | Sugar: 0 g

10. Sweet Potato Breakfast Skillet

Prep time: 10 min | Cook time: 20 min | Servings: 4

Ingredients:

- 2 medium sweet potatoes, peeled and diced
- 1 red bell pepper, diced
- 1 green bell pepper, diced
- 1 small onion, diced
- 2 tablespoons olive oil
- 1 teaspoon paprika
- 1 teaspoon garlic powder
- Salt and pepper to taste
- 4 eggs

Instructions:

1. Preheat air fryer to 200 degrees Celsius.
2. Toss sweet potatoes, bell peppers, and onion with olive oil, paprika, garlic powder, salt, and pepper.
3. Spread the vegetables in the air fryer basket.
4. Cook for 15 minutes, shaking the basket halfway through.
5. In the last 5 minutes, make small wells in the hash and crack an egg into each well.
6. Continue cooking until eggs are set.
7. Serve immediately.

Nutrition Facts (per serving): Calories: 230 kcal | Protein: 7 g | Carbs: 28 g | Fat: 10 g | Fiber: 5 g | Sugar: 8 g

11. Zucchini and Cheese Frittata

Prep time: 10 min | Cook time: 20 min | Servings: 6

Ingredients:

- 6 eggs
- 1 cup shredded zucchini
- 1/2 cup shredded cheddar cheese
- 1/4 cup chopped green onions
- Salt and pepper to taste
- 1 tablespoon olive oil

Instructions:

1. Preheat air fryer to 180 degrees Celsius.
2. In a large bowl, beat the eggs and season with salt and pepper.
3. Add shredded zucchini, cheddar cheese, and green onions. Mix well.
4. Heat olive oil in a pan over medium heat.

5. Pour the egg mixture into the pan and cook for 3-4 minutes until the edges start to set.
6. Transfer the pan to the air fryer and cook for 15 minutes or until the frittata is fully set and golden brown.
7. Allow to cool slightly before slicing and serving.

Nutrition Facts (per serving): Calories: 150 kcal | Protein: 10 g | Carbs: 2 g | Fat: 11 g | Fiber: 1 g | Sugar: 1 g

12. Protein-Packed Pancakes

Prep time: 10 min | Cook time: 15 min | Servings: 4

Ingredients:
- 1 cup rolled oats
- 1/2 cup cottage cheese
- 1/2 cup egg whites
- 1 teaspoon vanilla extract
- 1/2 teaspoon baking powder
- 1/4 teaspoon cinnamon
- 1/4 teaspoon salt

Instructions:
1. Preheat air fryer to 180 degrees Celsius.
2. In a blender, combine rolled oats, cottage cheese, egg whites, vanilla extract, baking powder, cinnamon, and salt. Blend until smooth.
3. Pour the batter into a greased air fryer-safe pan.
4. Cook for 15 minutes or until the pancakes are set and golden brown.
5. Allow to cool slightly before slicing and serving.

Nutrition Facts (per serving): Calories: 180 kcal | Protein: 15 g | Carbs: 24 g | Fat: 4 g | Fiber: 4 g | Sugar: 2 g

13. Air Fryer French Toast Sticks

Prep time: 10 min | Cook time: 10 min | Servings: 4

Ingredients:
- 4 slices whole grain bread
- 2 eggs
- 1/2 cup almond milk
- 1 teaspoon vanilla extract
- 1/2 teaspoon cinnamon
- 1 tablespoon honey
- Cooking spray

Instructions:
1. Preheat air fryer to 180 degrees Celsius.
2. In a bowl, whisk together eggs, almond milk, vanilla extract, cinnamon, and honey.
3. Cut bread slices into sticks and dip them into the egg mixture, ensuring they are well coated.

4. Spray the air fryer basket with cooking spray.
5. Arrange the bread sticks in a single layer in the basket.
6. Cook for 10 minutes, flipping halfway through, until golden brown and crispy.
7. Serve warm with your favorite toppings.

Nutrition Facts (per serving): Calories: 220 kcal | Protein: 8 g | Carbs: 30 g | Fat: 8 g | Fiber: 4 g | Sugar: 10 g

14. Mushroom and Spinach Breakfast Quiche

□□□Prep time: 15 min | Cook time: 25 min | Servings: 6

Ingredients:

- 1 pre-made whole grain pie crust
- 6 eggs
- 1 cup sliced mushrooms
- 1 cup chopped spinach
- 1/2 cup shredded Swiss cheese
- 1/2 cup almond milk
- Salt and pepper to taste

Instructions:

1. Preheat air fryer to 180 degrees Celsius.
2. In a bowl, beat the eggs and mix in almond milk, salt, and pepper.
3. Add mushrooms, spinach, and Swiss cheese to the egg mixture. Stir well.
4. Pour the filling into the pie crust.
5. Place the quiche in the air fryer and cook for 25 minutes or until the filling is set and the crust is golden brown.
6. Allow to cool slightly before slicing and serving.

Nutrition Facts (per serving): Calories: 230 kcal | Protein: 10 g | Carbs: 18 g | Fat: 14 g | Fiber: 2 g | Sugar: 1 g

15. Chia Seed Pudding

□□□Prep time: 5 min | Chill time: 4 hours | Servings: 4

Ingredients:

- 1/2 cup chia seeds
- 2 cups unsweetened almond milk
- 1 tablespoon honey
- 1 teaspoon vanilla extract
- Fresh berries for topping

Instructions:

1. In a bowl, whisk together chia seeds, almond milk, honey, and vanilla extract.
2. Cover and refrigerate for at least 4 hours or overnight, stirring occasionally to prevent clumping.
3. Before serving, give the pudding a good stir.
4. Divide into serving bowls and top with fresh berries.

Nutrition Facts (per serving): Calories: 150 kcal | Protein: 5 g | Carbs: 20 g | Fat: 7 g | Fiber: 10 g | Sugar: 6 g

16. Air Fryer Breakfast Potatoes

Prep time: 10 min | Cook time: 20 min | Servings: 4

Ingredients:

- 4 medium potatoes, diced
- 1 tablespoon olive oil
- 1 teaspoon garlic powder
- 1 teaspoon paprika
- 1/2 teaspoon salt
- 1/4 teaspoon black pepper

Instructions:

1. Preheat air fryer to 200 degrees Celsius.
2. In a bowl, toss diced potatoes with olive oil, garlic powder, paprika, salt, and pepper.
3. Spread the potatoes in the air fryer basket in a single layer.
4. Cook for 20 minutes, shaking the basket halfway through, until potatoes are crispy and golden brown.
5. Serve immediately.

Nutrition Facts (per serving): Calories: 180 kcal | Protein: 4 g | Carbs: 35 g | Fat: 4 g | Fiber: 4 g | Sugar: 2 g

17. Healthy Breakfast Sandwich

Prep time: 10 min | Cook time: 10 min | Servings: 2

Ingredients:

- 2 whole grain English muffins, split and toasted
- 2 eggs
- 2 slices turkey bacon
- 1/2 avocado, sliced
- 1/2 cup spinach leaves
- Salt and pepper to taste

Instructions:

1. Preheat air fryer to 180 degrees Celsius.
2. Cook turkey bacon in the air fryer for 8-10 minutes until crispy.
3. While the bacon cooks, cook the eggs in a pan to your desired doneness.
4. Toast the English muffins in the air fryer for 1-2 minutes.
5. Assemble the sandwich by layering spinach, avocado slices, cooked egg, and turkey bacon on the bottom half of each English muffin. Top with the other half.
6. Serve immediately.

Nutrition Facts (per sandwich): Calories: 250 kcal | Protein: 14 g | Carbs: 28 g | Fat: 10 g | Fiber: 6 g | Sugar: 3 g

18. Egg and Veggie Breakfast Cups

Prep time: 10 min | Cook time: 20 min | Servings: 6

Ingredients:

- 6 eggs
- 1/2 cup diced bell peppers
- 1/2 cup chopped spinach
- 1/4 cup shredded cheddar cheese
- Salt and pepper to taste

Instructions:

1. Preheat air fryer to 175 degrees Celsius.
2. In a bowl, beat the eggs and season with salt and pepper.
3. Add bell peppers, spinach, and cheddar cheese to the eggs. Mix well.
4. Grease a muffin tin and pour the egg mixture evenly into the cups.
5. Place the muffin tin in the air fryer and cook for 20 minutes or until the eggs are set.
6. Allow to cool slightly before serving.

Nutrition Facts (per cup): Calories: 90 kcal | Protein: 7 g | Carbs: 1 g | Fat: 6 g | Fiber: 0.5 g | Sugar: 1 g

19. Air Fryer Granola

Prep time: 10 min | Cook time: 15 min | Servings: 8

Ingredients:

- 2 cups rolled oats
- 1/2 cup chopped nuts (almonds, walnuts)
- 1/4 cup honey
- 1/4 cup coconut oil, melted
- 1 teaspoon vanilla extract
- 1/2 teaspoon cinnamon
- 1/4 teaspoon salt

Instructions:

1. Preheat air fryer to 160 degrees Celsius.
2. In a large bowl, mix oats, chopped nuts, honey, coconut oil, vanilla extract, cinnamon, and salt.
3. Spread the mixture evenly in the air fryer basket.
4. Cook for 15 minutes, stirring every 5 minutes, until the granola is golden brown and crispy.
5. Allow to cool before serving.

Nutrition Facts (per serving): Calories: 200 kcal | Protein: 4 g | Carbs: 27 g | Fat: 10 g | Fiber: 4 g | Sugar: 10 g

20. Banana Nut Muffins

Prep time: 10 min | Cook time: 15 min | Servings: 12

Ingredients:

- 1 1/2 cups whole wheat flour

- 1/2 cup rolled oats
- 1 teaspoon baking powder
- 1/2 teaspoon baking soda
- 1/2 teaspoon cinnamon
- 1/4 teaspoon salt
- 2 ripe bananas, mashed
- 1/3 cup honey
- 1/4 cup unsweetened applesauce
- 1/4 cup almond milk
- 1 teaspoon vanilla extract
- 1/4 cup chopped walnuts

Instructions:

1. Preheat air fryer to 175 degrees Celsius.
2. In a large bowl, mix flour, oats, baking powder, baking soda, cinnamon, and salt.
3. In another bowl, combine mashed bananas, honey, applesauce, almond milk, and vanilla extract.
4. Add the wet ingredients to the dry ingredients and mix until just combined.
5. Fold in chopped walnuts.
6. Spoon the batter into greased silicone muffin cups, filling each about 3/4 full.
7. Place the cups in the air fryer basket and cook for 15 minutes or until a toothpick inserted into the muffins comes out clean.
8. Allow to cool slightly before serving.

Nutrition Facts (per muffin): Calories: 150 kcal | Protein: 4 g | Carbs: 30 g | Fat: 3 g | Fiber: 4 g | Sugar: 12 g

Grains and Legumes Recipes

21. Quinoa Stuffed Bell Peppers

☐☐☐Prep time: 15 min | Cook time: 20 min | Servings: 4

Ingredients:

- 4 bell peppers, tops removed and seeded
- 1 cup cooked quinoa
- 1/2 cup black beans, rinsed and drained
- 1/2 cup corn kernels
- 1/2 cup diced tomatoes
- 1/4 cup chopped onions
- 1 teaspoon cumin
- 1 teaspoon chili powder
- 1/2 cup shredded cheddar cheese (optional)
- Salt and pepper to taste

Instructions:

1. Preheat air fryer to 180 degrees Celsius.
2. In a large bowl, mix cooked quinoa, black beans, corn, tomatoes, onions, cumin, chili powder, salt, and pepper.

3. Stuff the bell peppers with the quinoa mixture.
4. Place the stuffed peppers in the air fryer basket.
5. Cook for 20 minutes or until the peppers are tender.
6. If using, sprinkle cheddar cheese on top of the peppers in the last 5 minutes of cooking.
7. Serve warm.

Nutrition Facts (per serving): Calories: 200 kcal | Protein: 8 g | Carbs: 35 g | Fat: 5 g | Fiber: 10 g | Sugar: 8 g

22. Brown Rice and Veggie Stir-Fry

Prep time: 10 min | Cook time: 15 min | Servings: 4

Ingredients:

- 2 cups cooked brown rice
- 1 cup broccoli florets
- 1 red bell pepper, sliced
- 1 carrot, sliced
- 1/2 cup snap peas
- 2 tablespoons soy sauce (low sodium)
- 1 tablespoon olive oil
- 1 teaspoon garlic powder
- 1 teaspoon ginger powder
- Salt and pepper to taste

Instructions:

1. Preheat air fryer to 180 degrees Celsius.
2. In a large bowl, toss broccoli, bell pepper, carrot, and snap peas with olive oil, garlic powder, ginger powder, salt, and pepper.
3. Spread the vegetables in the air fryer basket and cook for 10 minutes, shaking the basket halfway through.
4. In a large skillet, combine cooked brown rice and air-fried vegetables.
5. Add soy sauce and stir-fry for an additional 5 minutes.
6. Serve warm.

Nutrition Facts (per serving): Calories: 250 kcal | Protein: 6 g | Carbs: 45 g | Fat: 5 g | Fiber: 5 g | Sugar: 4 g

23. Air Fryer Chickpea Snacks

Prep time: 5 min | Cook time: 15 min | Servings: 4

Ingredients:

- 1 can chickpeas, rinsed and drained
- 1 tablespoon olive oil
- 1 teaspoon smoked paprika
- 1/2 teaspoon garlic powder
- 1/2 teaspoon cumin

- Salt and pepper to taste

Instructions:

1. Preheat air fryer to 200 degrees Celsius.
2. In a large bowl, toss chickpeas with olive oil, smoked paprika, garlic powder, cumin, salt, and pepper.
3. Spread the chickpeas in the air fryer basket in a single layer.
4. Cook for 15 minutes, shaking the basket halfway through, until chickpeas are crispy.
5. Serve as a snack or topping for salads.

Nutrition Facts (per serving): Calories: 150 kcal | Protein: 6 g | Carbs: 20 g | Fat: 5 g | Fiber: 6 g | Sugar: 1 g

24. Lentil and Spinach Curry

Prep time: 10 min | Cook time: 30 min | Servings: 4

Ingredients:

- 1 cup lentils, rinsed
- 4 cups vegetable broth
- 1 onion, chopped
- 2 garlic cloves, minced
- 1 tablespoon olive oil
- 1 teaspoon turmeric
- 1 teaspoon cumin
- 1 teaspoon coriander
- 1/2 teaspoon chili powder
- 2 cups fresh spinach
- Salt and pepper to taste

Instructions:

1. Heat olive oil in a large pot over medium heat. Add chopped onion and garlic, sauté until translucent.
2. Add turmeric, cumin, coriander, and chili powder, cooking for 1 minute.
3. Add lentils and vegetable broth. Bring to a boil, then reduce heat and simmer for 25 minutes or until lentils are tender.
4. Stir in fresh spinach and cook for another 5 minutes.
5. Season with salt and pepper to taste.
6. Serve warm.

Nutrition Facts (per serving): Calories: 220 kcal | Protein: 12 g | Carbs: 30 g | Fat: 5 g | Fiber: 10 g | Sugar: 4 g

25. Quinoa and Black Bean Burgers

Prep time: 15 min | Cook time: 10 min | Servings: 6

Ingredients:

- 1 cup cooked quinoa

- 1 can black beans, rinsed and drained
- 1/2 cup breadcrumbs
- 1/4 cup chopped onions
- 1/4 cup chopped bell peppers
- 1 teaspoon cumin
- 1 teaspoon garlic powder
- 1 egg, beaten
- Salt and pepper to taste

Instructions:

1. In a large bowl, mash black beans with a fork.
2. Add cooked quinoa, breadcrumbs, onions, bell peppers, cumin, garlic powder, beaten egg, salt, and pepper. Mix until well combined.
3. Form the mixture into 6 patties.
4. Preheat air fryer to 180 degrees Celsius.
5. Place patties in the air fryer basket in a single layer.
6. Cook for 10 minutes, flipping halfway through, until patties are crispy and heated through.
7. Serve warm on whole grain buns with your favorite toppings.

Nutrition Facts (per patty): Calories: 180 kcal | Protein: 7 g | Carbs: 30 g | Fat: 4 g | Fiber: 8 g | Sugar: 2 g

26. Brown Rice Pilaf

Prep time: 10 min | Cook time: 25 min | Servings: 4

Ingredients:

- 1 cup brown rice
- 2 cups vegetable broth
- 1/4 cup chopped onions
- 1/4 cup diced carrots
- 1/4 cup diced celery
- 1 tablespoon olive oil
- 1 teaspoon thyme
- Salt and pepper to taste

Instructions:

1. Heat olive oil in a large pot over medium heat. Add onions, carrots, and celery, sauté until softened.
2. Add brown rice and thyme, cooking for 1-2 minutes to toast the rice.
3. Add vegetable broth and bring to a boil. Reduce heat, cover, and simmer for 20-25 minutes or until rice is tender.
4. Fluff with a fork and season with salt and pepper to taste.
5. Serve warm.

Nutrition Facts (per serving): Calories: 180 kcal | Protein: 4 g | Carbs: 35 g | Fat: 3 g | Fiber: 3 g | Sugar: 2 g

27. Air Fryer Falafel

Prep time: 15 min | Cook time: 15 min | Servings: 4

Ingredients:

- 1 can chickpeas, rinsed and drained
- 1/4 cup chopped onions
- 2 garlic cloves, minced
- 1/4 cup fresh parsley
- 1 teaspoon cumin
- 1 teaspoon coriander
- 1/2 teaspoon baking powder
- 2 tablespoons flour
- Salt and pepper to taste
- Cooking spray

Instructions:

1. In a food processor, combine chickpeas, onions, garlic, parsley, cumin, coriander, baking powder, flour, salt, and pepper. Process until well mixed but still slightly chunky.
2. Form the mixture into small balls.
3. Preheat air fryer to 180 degrees Celsius.
4. Spray the air fryer basket with cooking spray.
5. Arrange the falafel balls in the basket in a single layer.
6. Cook for 15 minutes, shaking the basket halfway through, until falafel are golden brown and crispy.
7. Serve warm with tahini sauce or in pita bread.

Nutrition Facts (per serving): Calories: 150 kcal | Protein: 5 g | Carbs: 20 g | Fat: 5 g | Fiber: 5 g | Sugar: 1 g

28. Lentil Soup

Prep time: 10 min | Cook time: 30 min | Servings: 4

Ingredients:

- 1 cup lentils, rinsed
- 4 cups vegetable broth
- 1 onion, chopped
- 2 carrots, diced
- 2 celery stalks, diced
- 2 garlic cloves, minced
- 1 tablespoon olive oil
- 1 teaspoon thyme
- 1 teaspoon cumin
- Salt and pepper to taste

Instructions:

1. Heat olive oil in a large pot over medium heat. Add onions, carrots, celery, and garlic, sauté until softened.
2. Add lentils, thyme, and cumin, cooking for 1-2 minutes.
3. Add vegetable broth and bring to a boil. Reduce heat and simmer for 25-30 minutes or until lentils are tender.
4. Season with salt and pepper to taste.
5. Serve warm.

Nutrition Facts (per serving): Calories: 200 kcal | Protein: 12 g | Carbs: 30 g | Fat: 5 g | Fiber: 10 g | Sugar: 4 g

29. Barley and Mushroom Risotto

Prep time: 10 min | Cook time: 30 min | Servings: 4

Ingredients:

- 1 cup pearl barley
- 4 cups vegetable broth
- 1 onion, chopped
- 2 garlic cloves, minced
- 1 cup sliced mushrooms
- 1 tablespoon olive oil
- 1/2 cup grated Parmesan cheese
- 1/4 cup chopped parsley
- Salt and pepper to taste

Instructions:

1. Heat olive oil in a large pot over medium heat. Add onions and garlic, sauté until translucent.
2. Add mushrooms and cook until softened.
3. Add barley and cook for 1-2 minutes to toast.
4. Gradually add vegetable broth, 1 cup at a time, stirring frequently and allowing each addition to be absorbed before adding the next.
5. Cook for 25-30 minutes or until barley is tender and creamy.
6. Stir in Parmesan cheese and parsley. Season with salt and pepper to taste.
7. Serve warm.

Nutrition Facts (per serving): Calories: 300 kcal | Protein: 10 g | Carbs: 50 g | Fat: 8 g | Fiber: 8 g | Sugar: 4 g

30. Air Fryer Tofu and Veggie Skewers

Prep time: 15 min | Cook time: 10 min | Servings: 4

Ingredients:

- 1 block firm tofu, pressed and cubed
- 1 red bell pepper, cubed
- 1 zucchini, sliced
- 1 red onion, cubed

- 1/4 cup soy sauce (low sodium)
- 2 tablespoons olive oil
- 1 tablespoon honey
- 1 teaspoon garlic powder
- 1 teaspoon ginger powder
- Skewers

Instructions:

1. In a bowl, mix soy sauce, olive oil, honey, garlic powder, and ginger powder.
2. Add tofu cubes and vegetables to the marinade. Let sit for 15 minutes.
3. Preheat air fryer to 200 degrees Celsius.
4. Thread tofu and vegetables onto skewers.
5. Place skewers in the air fryer basket in a single layer.
6. Cook for 10 minutes, flipping halfway through, until tofu is crispy and vegetables are tender.
7. Serve warm.

Nutrition Facts (per serving): Calories: 180 kcal | Protein: 10 g | Carbs: 10 g | Fat: 12 g | Fiber: 2 g | Sugar: 5 g

40

continua

ChatGPT

31. Quinoa Salad with Lemon Vinaigrette

Prep time: 15 min | Cook time: 15 min | Servings: 4

Ingredients:

- 1 cup cooked quinoa
- 1/2 cup diced cucumber
- 1/2 cup diced tomatoes
- 1/4 cup diced red onion
- 1/4 cup chopped fresh parsley
- 1/4 cup crumbled feta cheese
- 1/4 cup lemon juice
- 2 tablespoons olive oil
- Salt and pepper to taste

Instructions:

1. In a large bowl, combine cooked quinoa, cucumber, tomatoes, red onion, parsley, and feta cheese.
2. In a small bowl, whisk together lemon juice, olive oil, salt, and pepper.
3. Pour the vinaigrette over the salad and toss to combine.
4. Serve immediately or refrigerate until ready to serve.

Nutrition Facts (per serving): Calories: 220 kcal | Protein: 7 g | Carbs: 28 g | Fat: 10 g | Fiber: 4 g | Sugar: 3 g

32. Black Bean Tacos

Prep time: 10 min | Cook time: 10 min | Servings: 4

Ingredients:

- 1 can black beans, rinsed and drained
- 1 tablespoon olive oil
- 1 teaspoon cumin
- 1 teaspoon chili powder
- 8 small whole grain tortillas
- 1 cup shredded lettuce
- 1/2 cup diced tomatoes
- 1/4 cup diced red onion
- 1/4 cup chopped cilantro
- 1/4 cup shredded cheddar cheese (optional)
- Salt and pepper to taste

Instructions:

1. In a skillet, heat olive oil over medium heat. Add black beans, cumin, chili powder, salt, and pepper. Cook for 5 minutes until heated through.
2. Warm tortillas in the air fryer at 180 degrees Celsius for 1-2 minutes.
3. Fill each tortilla with black beans, lettuce, tomatoes, red onion, cilantro, and cheddar cheese if using.
4. Serve immediately.

Nutrition Facts (per serving): Calories: 250 kcal | Protein: 9 g | Carbs: 35 g | Fat: 8 g | Fiber: 10 g | Sugar: 2 g

33. Split Pea Soup

Prep time: 10 min | Cook time: 30 min | Servings: 4

Ingredients:

- 1 cup split peas, rinsed
- 4 cups vegetable broth
- 1 onion, chopped
- 2 carrots, diced
- 2 celery stalks, diced
- 2 garlic cloves, minced
- 1 tablespoon olive oil
- 1 teaspoon thyme
- Salt and pepper to taste

Instructions:

1. Heat olive oil in a large pot over medium heat. Add onions, carrots, celery, and garlic, sauté until softened.

2. Add split peas, thyme, and vegetable broth. Bring to a boil, then reduce heat and simmer for 30 minutes or until peas are tender.
3. Season with salt and pepper to taste.
4. Serve warm.

Nutrition Facts (per serving): Calories: 200 kcal | Protein: 12 g | Carbs: 35 g | Fat: 3 g | Fiber: 10 g | Sugar: 5 g

34. Chickpea and Veggie Buddha Bowl

Prep time: 15 min | Cook time: 15 min | Servings: 4

Ingredients:

- 1 can chickpeas, rinsed and drained
- 1 cup cooked quinoa
- 1 cup roasted sweet potatoes
- 1 cup steamed broccoli
- 1/2 cup shredded carrots
- 1/4 cup sliced avocado
- 2 tablespoons olive oil
- 1 tablespoon tahini
- 1 tablespoon lemon juice
- 1 teaspoon garlic powder
- Salt and pepper to taste

Instructions:

1. Preheat air fryer to 200 degrees Celsius.
2. In a bowl, toss chickpeas with 1 tablespoon of olive oil, garlic powder, salt, and pepper.
3. Spread chickpeas in the air fryer basket and cook for 15 minutes, shaking halfway through, until crispy.
4. In a large bowl, combine cooked quinoa, roasted sweet potatoes, steamed broccoli, shredded carrots, and sliced avocado.
5. In a small bowl, whisk together remaining olive oil, tahini, lemon juice, salt, and pepper.
6. Drizzle dressing over the Buddha bowl and top with crispy chickpeas.
7. Serve immediately.

Nutrition Facts (per serving): Calories: 350 kcal | Protein: 12 g | Carbs: 45 g | Fat: 15 g | Fiber: 10 g | Sugar: 6 g

35. Air Fryer Bean and Cheese Quesadillas

Prep time: 10 min | Cook time: 10 min | Servings: 4

Ingredients:

- 8 small whole grain tortillas
- 1 can black beans, rinsed and drained
- 1 cup shredded cheddar cheese
- 1/2 cup salsa

- 1/4 cup chopped cilantro
- Cooking spray

Instructions:

1. Preheat air fryer to 180 degrees Celsius.
2. In a bowl, mix black beans, cheddar cheese, salsa, and cilantro.
3. Spread the mixture evenly on 4 tortillas, then top with the remaining tortillas to form quesadillas.
4. Spray the air fryer basket with cooking spray.
5. Place the quesadillas in the basket in a single layer.
6. Cook for 10 minutes, flipping halfway through, until golden brown and crispy.
7. Cut into wedges and serve warm.

Nutrition Facts (per serving): Calories: 300 kcal | Protein: 12 g | Carbs: 40 g | Fat: 12 g | Fiber: 8 g | Sugar: 2 g

36. Lentil and Veggie Meatballs

Prep time: 15 min | Cook time: 20 min | Servings: 4

Ingredients:

- 1 cup cooked lentils
- 1/2 cup breadcrumbs
- 1/4 cup grated Parmesan cheese
- 1/4 cup chopped parsley
- 1 egg, beaten
- 1 garlic clove, minced
- 1 teaspoon oregano
- Salt and pepper to taste
- Cooking spray

Instructions:

1. In a large bowl, mix cooked lentils, breadcrumbs, Parmesan cheese, parsley, beaten egg, minced garlic, oregano, salt, and pepper.
2. Form the mixture into small meatballs.
3. Preheat air fryer to 180 degrees Celsius.
4. Spray the air fryer basket with cooking spray.
5. Arrange the meatballs in the basket in a single layer.
6. Cook for 15-20 minutes, shaking halfway through, until golden brown and cooked through.
7. Serve warm with your favorite sauce.

Nutrition Facts (per serving): Calories: 200 kcal | Protein: 12 g | Carbs: 30 g | Fat: 5 g | Fiber: 10 g | Sugar: 2 g

37. Air Fryer Stuffed Zucchini Boats

Prep time: 15 min | Cook time: 15 min | Servings: 4

Ingredients:

- 2 large zucchinis, halved lengthwise and seeded

- 1 cup cooked quinoa
- 1/2 cup diced tomatoes
- 1/4 cup chopped onions
- 1/4 cup crumbled feta cheese
- 1 tablespoon olive oil
- 1 teaspoon Italian seasoning
- Salt and pepper to taste

Instructions:
1. Preheat air fryer to 180 degrees Celsius.
2. In a large bowl, mix cooked quinoa, diced tomatoes, onions, feta cheese, olive oil, Italian seasoning, salt, and pepper.
3. Spoon the mixture into the zucchini halves.
4. Place the stuffed zucchinis in the air fryer basket.
5. Cook for 15 minutes or until the zucchinis are tender.
6. Serve warm.

Nutrition Facts (per serving): Calories: 150 kcal | Protein: 6 g | Carbs: 20 g | Fat: 7 g | Fiber: 3 g | Sugar: 4 g

38. Quinoa Breakfast Porridge

Prep time: 5 min | Cook time: 15 min | Servings: 4
Ingredients:
- 1 cup cooked quinoa
- 1 cup almond milk
- 1 tablespoon honey
- 1 teaspoon vanilla extract
- 1/2 teaspoon cinnamon
- Fresh berries for topping

Instructions:
1. In a pot, combine cooked quinoa, almond milk, honey, vanilla extract, and cinnamon.
2. Bring to a boil, then reduce heat and simmer for 5-10 minutes until thickened.
3. Divide into bowls and top with fresh berries.
4. Serve warm.

Nutrition Facts (per serving): Calories: 180 kcal | Protein: 6 g | Carbs: 30 g | Fat: 4 g | Fiber: 4 g | Sugar: 8 g

39. Three-Bean Salad

Prep time: 10 min | Cook time: 0 min | Servings: 4
Ingredients:
- 1 can black beans, rinsed and drained
- 1 can kidney beans, rinsed and drained
- 1 can chickpeas, rinsed and drained

- 1/2 cup diced red onion
- 1/2 cup diced bell pepper
- 1/4 cup chopped cilantro
- 1/4 cup olive oil
- 1/4 cup red wine vinegar
- 1 teaspoon cumin
- Salt and pepper to taste

Instructions:

1. In a large bowl, combine black beans, kidney beans, chickpeas, red onion, bell pepper, and cilantro.
2. In a small bowl, whisk together olive oil, red wine vinegar, cumin, salt, and pepper.
3. Pour the dressing over the salad and toss to combine.
4. Serve immediately or refrigerate until ready to serve.

Nutrition Facts (per serving): Calories: 250 kcal | Protein: 10 g | Carbs: 35 g | Fat: 10 g | Fiber: 10 g | Sugar: 3 g

40. Chickpea and Avocado Salad

☐☐☐Prep time: 10 min | Cook time: 0 min | Servings: 4

Ingredients:

- 1 can chickpeas, rinsed and drained
- 1 avocado, diced
- 1/2 cup cherry tomatoes, halved
- 1/4 cup diced red onion
- 1/4 cup chopped cilantro
- 1 tablespoon olive oil
- 1 tablespoon lemon juice
- Salt and pepper to taste

Instructions:

1. In a large bowl, combine chickpeas, avocado, cherry tomatoes, red onion, and cilantro.
2. In a small bowl, whisk together olive oil, lemon juice, salt, and pepper.
3. Pour the dressing over the salad and toss to combine.
4. Serve immediately.

Nutrition Facts (per serving): Calories: 220 kcal | Protein: 6 g | Carbs: 25 g | Fat: 12 g | Fiber: 8 g | Sugar: 3 g

41. Air Fryer Veggie Samosas

☐☐☐Prep time: 20 min | Cook time: 15 min | Servings: 4

Ingredients:

- 1 cup mashed potatoes
- 1/2 cup green peas
- 1/4 cup diced carrots
- 1/4 cup diced onions

- 1 teaspoon cumin seeds
- 1 teaspoon garam masala
- 1 teaspoon turmeric
- 1 tablespoon olive oil
- 8 small whole wheat tortillas
- Cooking spray
- Salt and pepper to taste

Instructions:

1. In a pan, heat olive oil over medium heat. Add cumin seeds, onions, carrots, and peas, sauté until vegetables are tender.
2. Add mashed potatoes, garam masala, turmeric, salt, and pepper. Mix well and cook for 2-3 minutes.
3. Cut tortillas in half and fold each half into a cone shape. Fill with the veggie mixture and seal the edges with a little water.
4. Preheat air fryer to 180 degrees Celsius.
5. Spray the samosas with cooking spray and place in the air fryer basket.
6. Cook for 10-15 minutes, flipping halfway through, until golden brown and crispy.
7. Serve warm with chutney.

Nutrition Facts (per serving): Calories: 180 kcal | Protein: 4 g | Carbs: 28 g | Fat: 5 g | Fiber: 6 g | Sugar: 2 g

42. Black Bean and Corn Salsa

☐☐☐Prep time: 10 min | Cook time: 0 min | Servings: 4

Ingredients:

- 1 can black beans, rinsed and drained
- 1 cup corn kernels
- 1/2 cup diced tomatoes
- 1/4 cup diced red onion
- 1/4 cup chopped cilantro
- 1 tablespoon lime juice
- 1 tablespoon olive oil
- Salt and pepper to taste

Instructions:

1. In a large bowl, combine black beans, corn, tomatoes, red onion, and cilantro.
2. In a small bowl, whisk together lime juice, olive oil, salt, and pepper.
3. Pour the dressing over the salsa and toss to combine.
4. Serve immediately or refrigerate until ready to serve.

Nutrition Facts (per serving): Calories: 120 kcal | Protein: 4 g | Carbs: 24 g | Fat: 3 g | Fiber: 6 g | Sugar: 2 g

43. Quinoa and Veggie Stir-Fry

☐☐☐Prep time: 10 min | Cook time: 15 min | Servings: 4

Ingredients:

- 2 cups cooked quinoa
- 1 cup broccoli florets
- 1 red bell pepper, sliced
- 1 carrot, sliced
- 1/2 cup snap peas
- 2 tablespoons soy sauce (low sodium)
- 1 tablespoon olive oil
- 1 teaspoon garlic powder
- 1 teaspoon ginger powder
- Salt and pepper to taste

Instructions:

1. Preheat air fryer to 180 degrees Celsius.
2. In a large bowl, toss broccoli, bell pepper, carrot, and snap peas with olive oil, garlic powder, ginger powder, salt, and pepper.
3. Spread the vegetables in the air fryer basket and cook for 10 minutes, shaking the basket halfway through.
4. In a large skillet, combine cooked quinoa and air-fried vegetables.
5. Add soy sauce and stir-fry for an additional 5 minutes.
6. Serve warm.

Nutrition Facts (per serving): Calories: 250 kcal | Protein: 8 g | Carbs: 40 g | Fat: 6 g | Fiber: 8 g | Sugar: 6 g

44. Red Lentil Dhal

Prep time: 10 min | Cook time: 25 min | Servings: 4

Ingredients:

- 1 cup red lentils, rinsed
- 4 cups water
- 1 onion, chopped
- 2 garlic cloves, minced
- 1 tablespoon olive oil
- 1 teaspoon turmeric
- 1 teaspoon cumin
- 1 teaspoon coriander
- 1/2 teaspoon chili powder
- Salt and pepper to taste

Instructions:

1. Heat olive oil in a large pot over medium heat. Add onions and garlic, sauté until translucent.
2. Add turmeric, cumin, coriander, and chili powder, cooking for 1 minute.
3. Add lentils and water. Bring to a boil, then reduce heat and simmer for 20 minutes or until lentils are tender.

4. Season with salt and pepper to taste.
5. Serve warm.

Nutrition Facts (per serving): Calories: 220 kcal | Protein: 12 g | Carbs: 35 g | Fat: 4 g | Fiber: 10 g | Sugar: 4 g

45. Air Fryer Edamame

□□□Prep time: 5 min | Cook time: 10 min | Servings: 4

Ingredients:
- 2 cups frozen edamame
- 1 tablespoon olive oil
- 1 teaspoon sea salt

Instructions:
1. Preheat air fryer to 180 degrees Celsius.
2. In a large bowl, toss edamame with olive oil and sea salt.
3. Spread edamame in the air fryer basket in a single layer.
4. Cook for 10 minutes, shaking the basket halfway through.
5. Serve warm.

Nutrition Facts (per serving): Calories: 100 kcal | Protein: 8 g | Carbs: 8 g | Fat: 4 g | Fiber: 4 g | Sugar: 1 g

46. Air Fryer Brussels Sprouts

□□□Prep time: 10 min | Cook time: 15 min | Servings: 4

Ingredients:
- 1 pound Brussels sprouts, trimmed and halved
- 2 tablespoons olive oil
- 1 teaspoon garlic powder
- 1 teaspoon onion powder
- Salt and pepper to taste

Instructions:
1. Preheat air fryer to 200 degrees Celsius.
2. In a large bowl, toss Brussels sprouts with olive oil, garlic powder, onion powder, salt, and pepper.
3. Spread Brussels sprouts in the air fryer basket in a single layer.
4. Cook for 15 minutes, shaking the basket halfway through, until golden brown and crispy.
5. Serve warm.

Nutrition Facts (per serving): Calories: 120 kcal | Protein: 4 g | Carbs: 10 g | Fat: 8 g | Fiber: 4 g | Sugar: 2 g

Sides and Vegetable Recipes

47. Garlic Parmesan Asparagus

Prep time: 5 min | Cook time: 10 min | Servings: 4

Ingredients:

- 1 pound asparagus, trimmed
- 2 tablespoons olive oil
- 1/4 cup grated Parmesan cheese
- 1 teaspoon garlic powder
- Salt and pepper to taste

Instructions:

1. Preheat air fryer to 200 degrees Celsius.
2. In a large bowl, toss asparagus with olive oil, Parmesan cheese, garlic powder, salt, and pepper.
3. Spread asparagus in the air fryer basket in a single layer.
4. Cook for 10 minutes, shaking the basket halfway through, until tender and crispy.
5. Serve warm.

Nutrition Facts (per serving): Calories: 120 kcal | Protein: 4 g | Carbs: 6 g | Fat: 10 g | Fiber: 3 g | Sugar: 2 g

48. Air Fryer Sweet Potato Fries

Prep time: 10 min | Cook time: 15 min | Servings: 4

Ingredients:

- 2 large sweet potatoes, peeled and cut into fries
- 2 tablespoons olive oil
- 1 teaspoon paprika
- 1 teaspoon garlic powder
- Salt and pepper to taste

Instructions:

1. Preheat air fryer to 200 degrees Celsius.
2. In a large bowl, toss sweet potato fries with olive oil, paprika, garlic powder, salt, and pepper.
3. Spread fries in the air fryer basket in a single layer.
4. Cook for 15 minutes, shaking the basket halfway through, until golden brown and crispy.
5. Serve warm.

Nutrition Facts (per serving): Calories: 150 kcal | Protein: 2 g | Carbs: 30 g | Fat: 5 g | Fiber: 5 g | Sugar: 8 g

49. Roasted Cauliflower

Prep time: 5 min | Cook time: 15 min | Servings: 4

Ingredients:

- 1 head cauliflower, cut into florets
- 2 tablespoons olive oil
- 1 teaspoon garlic powder
- 1 teaspoon paprika
- Salt and pepper to taste

Instructions:

1. Preheat air fryer to 200 degrees Celsius.
2. In a large bowl, toss cauliflower florets with olive oil, garlic powder, paprika, salt, and pepper.
3. Spread cauliflower in the air fryer basket in a single layer.
4. Cook for 15 minutes, shaking the basket halfway through, until golden brown and crispy.
5. Serve warm.

Nutrition Facts (per serving): Calories: 100 kcal | Protein: 3 g | Carbs: 10 g | Fat: 5 g | Fiber: 3 g | Sugar: 3 g

50. Air Fryer Zucchini Chips

Prep time: 10 min | Cook time: 10 min | Servings: 4

Ingredients:

- 2 zucchinis, thinly sliced
- 2 tablespoons olive oil
- 1/4 cup grated Parmesan cheese

- 1 teaspoon garlic powder
- Salt and pepper to taste

Instructions:

1. Preheat air fryer to 200 degrees Celsius.
2. In a large bowl, toss zucchini slices with olive oil, Parmesan cheese, garlic powder, salt, and pepper.
3. Spread zucchini slices in the air fryer basket in a single layer.
4. Cook for 10 minutes, shaking the basket halfway through, until golden brown and crispy.
5. Serve warm.

Nutrition Facts (per serving): Calories: 120 kcal | Protein: 4 g | Carbs: 6 g | Fat: 10 g | Fiber: 2 g | Sugar: 3 g

40

continua

ChatGPT

51. Green Bean Almondine

☐☐☐Prep time: 5 min | Cook time: 10 min | Servings: 4

Ingredients:

- 1 pound green beans, trimmed
- 2 tablespoons olive oil
- 1/4 cup sliced almonds
- 1 garlic clove, minced
- Juice of 1 lemon
- Salt and pepper to taste

Instructions:

1. Preheat air fryer to 200 degrees Celsius.
2. In a large bowl, toss green beans with olive oil, sliced almonds, minced garlic, lemon juice, salt, and pepper.
3. Spread green beans in the air fryer basket in a single layer.
4. Cook for 10 minutes, shaking the basket halfway through, until green beans are tender and almonds are toasted.
5. Serve warm.

Nutrition Facts (per serving): Calories: 140 kcal | Protein: 4 g | Carbs: 10 g | Fat: 10 g | Fiber: 4 g | Sugar: 2 g

52. Air Fryer Stuffed Mushrooms

☐☐☐Prep time: 15 min | Cook time: 10 min | Servings: 4

Ingredients:

- 12 large mushrooms, stems removed
- 1/4 cup breadcrumbs
- 1/4 cup grated Parmesan cheese
- 2 tablespoons chopped parsley

- 1 garlic clove, minced
- 2 tablespoons olive oil
- Salt and pepper to taste

Instructions:

1. Preheat air fryer to 180 degrees Celsius.
2. In a bowl, mix breadcrumbs, Parmesan cheese, parsley, minced garlic, olive oil, salt, and pepper.
3. Spoon the filling into the mushroom caps.
4. Place the stuffed mushrooms in the air fryer basket in a single layer.
5. Cook for 10 minutes, until the mushrooms are tender and the filling is golden brown.
6. Serve warm.

Nutrition Facts (per serving): Calories: 100 kcal | Protein: 5 g | Carbs: 10 g | Fat: 4 g | Fiber: 2 g | Sugar: 2 g

53. Balsamic Glazed Carrots

Prep time: 10 min | Cook time: 15 min | Servings: 4

Ingredients:

- 1 pound carrots, peeled and sliced
- 2 tablespoons balsamic vinegar
- 2 tablespoons olive oil
- 1 tablespoon honey
- 1 teaspoon thyme
- Salt and pepper to taste

Instructions:

1. Preheat air fryer to 200 degrees Celsius.
2. In a large bowl, toss carrots with balsamic vinegar, olive oil, honey, thyme, salt, and pepper.
3. Spread carrots in the air fryer basket in a single layer.
4. Cook for 15 minutes, shaking the basket halfway through, until tender and caramelized.
5. Serve warm.

Nutrition Facts (per serving): Calories: 120 kcal | Protein: 1 g | Carbs: 20 g | Fat: 5 g | Fiber: 4 g | Sugar: 12 g

54. Crispy Kale Chips

Prep time: 5 min | Cook time: 10 min | Servings: 4

Ingredients:

- 1 bunch kale, stems removed and torn into pieces
- 2 tablespoons olive oil
- 1 teaspoon garlic powder
- 1 teaspoon paprika
- Salt and pepper to taste

Instructions:

1. Preheat air fryer to 180 degrees Celsius.

2. In a large bowl, toss kale pieces with olive oil, garlic powder, paprika, salt, and pepper.
3. Spread kale in the air fryer basket in a single layer.
4. Cook for 10 minutes, shaking the basket halfway through, until crispy.
5. Serve immediately.

Nutrition Facts (per serving): Calories: 70 kcal | Protein: 2 g | Carbs: 7 g | Fat: 5 g | Fiber: 3 g | Sugar: 1 g

55. Air Fryer Eggplant Parmesan

Prep time: 15 min | Cook time: 15 min | Servings: 4

Ingredients:
- 1 large eggplant, sliced into rounds
- 1 cup breadcrumbs
- 1/2 cup grated Parmesan cheese
- 2 eggs, beaten
- 1 cup marinara sauce
- 1 cup shredded mozzarella cheese
- Cooking spray
- Salt and pepper to taste

Instructions:
1. Preheat air fryer to 180 degrees Celsius.
2. In a shallow bowl, mix breadcrumbs and Parmesan cheese.
3. Dip eggplant slices into beaten eggs, then coat with breadcrumb mixture.
4. Spray the air fryer basket with cooking spray and place the eggplant slices in a single layer.
5. Cook for 10 minutes, flipping halfway through, until golden brown and crispy.
6. Top each eggplant slice with marinara sauce and shredded mozzarella cheese.
7. Cook for an additional 5 minutes until the cheese is melted and bubbly.
8. Serve warm.

Nutrition Facts (per serving): Calories: 250 kcal | Protein: 15 g | Carbs: 25 g | Fat: 10 g | Fiber: 7 g | Sugar: 5 g

56. Roasted Bell Peppers

Prep time: 5 min | Cook time: 15 min | Servings: 4

Ingredients:
- 4 bell peppers, sliced
- 2 tablespoons olive oil
- 1 teaspoon garlic powder
- 1 teaspoon dried oregano
- Salt and pepper to taste

Instructions:
1. Preheat air fryer to 200 degrees Celsius.
2. In a large bowl, toss bell peppers with olive oil, garlic powder, oregano, salt, and pepper.

3. Spread bell peppers in the air fryer basket in a single layer.
4. Cook for 15 minutes, shaking the basket halfway through, until tender and slightly charred.
5. Serve warm.

Nutrition Facts (per serving): Calories: 100 kcal | Protein: 1 g | Carbs: 8 g | Fat: 7 g | Fiber: 2 g | Sugar: 4 g

57. Air Fryer Broccoli with Lemon

□□□Prep time: 5 min | Cook time: 10 min | Servings: 4

Ingredients:

- 1 pound broccoli florets
- 2 tablespoons olive oil
- Juice of 1 lemon
- 1 teaspoon garlic powder
- Salt and pepper to taste

Instructions:

1. Preheat air fryer to 200 degrees Celsius.
2. In a large bowl, toss broccoli florets with olive oil, lemon juice, garlic powder, salt, and pepper.
3. Spread broccoli in the air fryer basket in a single layer.
4. Cook for 10 minutes, shaking the basket halfway through, until tender and slightly crispy.
5. Serve warm.

Nutrition Facts (per serving): Calories: 120 kcal | Protein: 3 g | Carbs: 10 g | Fat: 8 g | Fiber: 4 g | Sugar: 2 g

58. Spicy Roasted Chickpeas

□□□Prep time: 5 min | Cook time: 15 min | Servings: 4

Ingredients:

- 1 can chickpeas, rinsed and drained
- 2 tablespoons olive oil
- 1 teaspoon smoked paprika
- 1/2 teaspoon cayenne pepper
- 1/2 teaspoon garlic powder
- Salt and pepper to taste

Instructions:

1. Preheat air fryer to 200 degrees Celsius.
2. In a large bowl, toss chickpeas with olive oil, smoked paprika, cayenne pepper, garlic powder, salt, and pepper.
3. Spread chickpeas in the air fryer basket in a single layer.
4. Cook for 15 minutes, shaking the basket halfway through, until crispy.
5. Serve warm.

Nutrition Facts (per serving): Calories: 140 kcal | Protein: 6 g | Carbs: 20 g | Fat: 5 g | Fiber: 6 g | Sugar: 1 g

59. Cauliflower Rice

☐☐☐Prep time: 5 min | Cook time: 10 min | Servings: 4

Ingredients:

- 1 head cauliflower, grated into rice-sized pieces
- 2 tablespoons olive oil
- 1 teaspoon garlic powder
- 1 teaspoon onion powder
- Salt and pepper to taste

Instructions:

1. Preheat air fryer to 200 degrees Celsius.
2. In a large bowl, toss grated cauliflower with olive oil, garlic powder, onion powder, salt, and pepper.
3. Spread cauliflower in the air fryer basket in a single layer.
4. Cook for 10 minutes, shaking the basket halfway through, until tender and slightly crispy.
5. Serve warm.

Nutrition Facts (per serving): Calories: 70 kcal | Protein: 2 g | Carbs: 7 g | Fat: 5 g | Fiber: 3 g | Sugar: 2 g

60. Air Fryer Garlic Mushrooms

☐☐☐Prep time: 5 min | Cook time: 10 min | Servings: 4

Ingredients:

- 1 pound mushrooms, cleaned and halved
- 2 tablespoons olive oil
- 3 garlic cloves, minced
- 1 teaspoon dried thyme
- Salt and pepper to taste

Instructions:

1. Preheat air fryer to 200 degrees Celsius.
2. In a large bowl, toss mushrooms with olive oil, minced garlic, dried thyme, salt, and pepper.
3. Spread mushrooms in the air fryer basket in a single layer.
4. Cook for 10 minutes, shaking the basket halfway through, until tender and golden brown.
5. Serve warm.

Nutrition Facts (per serving): Calories: 100 kcal | Protein: 3 g | Carbs: 5 g | Fat: 8 g | Fiber: 2 g | Sugar: 2 g

61. Maple Glazed Butternut Squash

☐☐☐Prep time: 10 min | Cook time: 15 min | Servings: 4

Ingredients:

- 1 butternut squash, peeled and cubed
- 2 tablespoons maple syrup
- 2 tablespoons olive oil

- 1 teaspoon cinnamon
- Salt and pepper to taste

Instructions:

1. Preheat air fryer to 200 degrees Celsius.
2. In a large bowl, toss butternut squash cubes with maple syrup, olive oil, cinnamon, salt, and pepper.
3. Spread squash in the air fryer basket in a single layer.
4. Cook for 15 minutes, shaking the basket halfway through, until tender and caramelized.
5. Serve warm.

Nutrition Facts (per serving): Calories: 150 kcal | Protein: 1 g | Carbs: 30 g | Fat: 5 g | Fiber: 4 g | Sugar: 12 g

62. Air Fryer Avocado Fries

□□□Prep time: 10 min | Cook time: 10 min | Servings: 4

Ingredients:

- 2 ripe avocados, sliced
- 1/2 cup breadcrumbs
- 1/4 cup grated Parmesan cheese
- 2 eggs, beaten
- Cooking spray
- Salt and pepper to taste

Instructions:

1. Preheat air fryer to 200 degrees Celsius.
2. In a shallow bowl, mix breadcrumbs and Parmesan cheese.
3. Dip avocado slices into beaten eggs, then coat with breadcrumb mixture.
4. Spray the air fryer basket with cooking spray and place avocado slices in a single layer.
5. Cook for 10 minutes, flipping halfway through, until golden brown and crispy.
6. Serve warm with your favorite dipping sauce.

Nutrition Facts (per serving): Calories: 180 kcal | Protein: 4 g | Carbs: 12 g | Fat: 14 g | Fiber: 6 g | Sugar: 1 g

63. Roasted Beet Salad

□□□Prep time: 10 min | Cook time: 20 min | Servings: 4

Ingredients:

- 4 medium beets, peeled and diced
- 2 tablespoons olive oil
- 1 teaspoon thyme
- 1/4 cup crumbled goat cheese
- 1/4 cup chopped walnuts
- 2 tablespoons balsamic vinegar
- Salt and pepper to taste

Instructions:

1. Preheat air fryer to 200 degrees Celsius.
2. In a large bowl, toss beets with olive oil, thyme, salt, and pepper.
3. Spread beets in the air fryer basket in a single layer.
4. Cook for 20 minutes, shaking the basket halfway through, until tender and caramelized.
5. Transfer roasted beets to a salad bowl. Add goat cheese, walnuts, and balsamic vinegar. Toss to combine.
6. Serve immediately.

Nutrition Facts (per serving): Calories: 200 kcal | Protein: 5 g | Carbs: 20 g | Fat: 12 g | Fiber: 5 g | Sugar: 12 g

64. Air Fryer Okra

Prep time: 5 min | Cook time: 15 min | Servings: 4

Ingredients:
- 1 pound okra, trimmed
- 2 tablespoons olive oil
- 1 teaspoon smoked paprika
- 1 teaspoon garlic powder
- Salt and pepper to taste

Instructions:
1. Preheat air fryer to 200 degrees Celsius.
2. In a large bowl, toss okra with olive oil, smoked paprika, garlic powder, salt, and pepper.
3. Spread okra in the air fryer basket in a single layer.
4. Cook for 15 minutes, shaking the basket halfway through, until crispy and golden brown.
5. Serve warm.

Nutrition Facts (per serving): Calories: 100 kcal | Protein: 2 g | Carbs: 10 g | Fat: 7 g | Fiber: 4 g | Sugar: 2 g

65. Lemon Herb Roasted Radishes

Prep time: 5 min | Cook time: 15 min | Servings: 4

Ingredients:
- 1 pound radishes, halved
- 2 tablespoons olive oil
- Juice of 1 lemon
- 1 teaspoon dried thyme
- Salt and pepper to taste

Instructions:
1. Preheat air fryer to 200 degrees Celsius.
2. In a large bowl, toss radishes with olive oil, lemon juice, dried thyme, salt, and pepper.
3. Spread radishes in the air fryer basket in a single layer.
4. Cook for 15 minutes, shaking the basket halfway through, until tender and slightly crispy.
5. Serve warm.

Nutrition Facts (per serving): Calories: 90 kcal | Protein: 1 g | Carbs: 5 g | Fat: 7 g | Fiber: 2 g | Sugar: 2 g

66. Air Fryer Baby Carrots

Prep time: 5 min | Cook time: 15 min | Servings: 4

Ingredients:
- 1 pound baby carrots
- 2 tablespoons olive oil
- 1 teaspoon honey
- 1 teaspoon garlic powder
- Salt and pepper to taste

Instructions:
1. Preheat air fryer to 200 degrees Celsius.
2. In a large bowl, toss baby carrots with olive oil, honey, garlic powder, salt, and pepper.
3. Spread baby carrots in the air fryer basket in a single layer.
4. Cook for 15 minutes, shaking the basket halfway through, until tender and caramelized.
5. Serve warm.

Nutrition Facts (per serving): Calories: 110 kcal | Protein: 1 g | Carbs: 12 g | Fat: 7 g | Fiber: 4 g | Sugar: 6 g

67. Sautéed Spinach with Garlic

Prep time: 5 min | Cook time: 5 min | Servings: 4

Ingredients:
- 1 pound fresh spinach
- 2 tablespoons olive oil
- 3 garlic cloves, minced
- Salt and pepper to taste

Instructions:
1. Heat olive oil in a large skillet over medium heat. Add minced garlic and sauté for 1 minute until fragrant.
2. Add fresh spinach and cook for 3-5 minutes until wilted.
3. Season with salt and pepper to taste.
4. Serve immediately.

Nutrition Facts (per serving): Calories: 70 kcal | Protein: 2 g | Carbs: 3 g | Fat: 6 g | Fiber: 2 g | Sugar: 1 g

68. Air Fryer Cabbage Steaks

Prep time: 5 min | Cook time: 15 min | Servings: 4

Ingredients:
- 1 head cabbage, sliced into steaks

- 2 tablespoons olive oil
- 1 teaspoon garlic powder
- 1 teaspoon paprika
- Salt and pepper to taste

Instructions:

1. Preheat air fryer to 200 degrees Celsius.
2. In a large bowl, brush cabbage steaks with olive oil and season with garlic powder, paprika, salt, and pepper.
3. Place cabbage steaks in the air fryer basket in a single layer.
4. Cook for 15 minutes, flipping halfway through, until tender and slightly crispy.
5. Serve warm.

Nutrition Facts (per serving): Calories: 80 kcal | Protein: 2 g | Carbs: 8 g | Fat: 5 g | Fiber: 3 g | Sugar: 4 g

69. Roasted Artichoke Hearts

Prep time: 10 min | Cook time: 15 min | Servings: 4

Ingredients:

- 1 can artichoke hearts, drained and halved
- 2 tablespoons olive oil
- 1 teaspoon garlic powder
- 1 teaspoon dried thyme
- Salt and pepper to taste

Instructions:

1. Preheat air fryer to 200 degrees Celsius.
2. In a large bowl, toss artichoke hearts with olive oil, garlic powder, dried thyme, salt, and pepper.
3. Spread artichoke hearts in the air fryer basket in a single layer.
4. Cook for 15 minutes, shaking the basket halfway through, until tender and crispy.
5. Serve warm.

Nutrition Facts (per serving): Calories: 100 kcal | Protein: 2 g | Carbs: 8 g | Fat: 7 g | Fiber: 4 g | Sugar: 2 g

70. Air Fryer Bell Pepper Rings

Prep time: 10 min | Cook time: 10 min | Servings: 4

Ingredients:

- 2 bell peppers, sliced into rings
- 2 tablespoons olive oil
- 1 teaspoon garlic powder
- 1 teaspoon smoked paprika
- Salt and pepper to taste

Instructions:

1. Preheat air fryer to 200 degrees Celsius.

2. In a large bowl, toss bell pepper rings with olive oil, garlic powder, smoked paprika, salt, and pepper.
3. Spread bell pepper rings in the air fryer basket in a single layer.
4. Cook for 10 minutes, shaking the basket halfway through, until tender and slightly charred.
5. Serve warm.

Nutrition Facts (per serving): Calories: 80 kcal | Protein: 1 g | Carbs: 8 g | Fat: 5 g | Fiber: 2 g | Sugar: 4 g

Fish and Seafood Recipes

71. Lemon Garlic Air Fryer Salmon

□□□Prep time: 5 min | Cook time: 12 min | Servings: 4

Ingredients:
- 4 salmon fillets
- 2 tablespoons olive oil
- 2 tablespoons lemon juice
- 3 garlic cloves, minced
- Salt and pepper to taste
- Lemon wedges for serving

Instructions:
1. Preheat air fryer to 200 degrees Celsius.
2. In a small bowl, mix olive oil, lemon juice, minced garlic, salt, and pepper.
3. Brush the mixture over the salmon fillets.
4. Place the salmon fillets in the air fryer basket.
5. Cook for 12 minutes, or until the salmon is cooked through and flakes easily with a fork.
6. Serve with lemon wedges.

Nutrition Facts (per serving): Calories: 250 kcal | Protein: 23 g | Carbs: 2 g | Fat: 16 g | Fiber: 0 g | Sugar: 0 g

72. Crispy Air Fryer Shrimp

□□□Prep time: 10 min | Cook time: 10 min | Servings: 4

Ingredients:
- 1 pound large shrimp, peeled and deveined
- 1/2 cup breadcrumbs
- 1/4 cup grated Parmesan cheese
- 2 eggs, beaten
- 2 tablespoons olive oil
- 1 teaspoon garlic powder
- 1 teaspoon paprika
- Salt and pepper to taste

- Lemon wedges for serving

Instructions:

1. Preheat air fryer to 200 degrees Celsius.
2. In a shallow bowl, mix breadcrumbs, Parmesan cheese, garlic powder, paprika, salt, and pepper.
3. Dip each shrimp in the beaten eggs, then coat with the breadcrumb mixture.
4. Place the shrimp in the air fryer basket in a single layer.
5. Cook for 10 minutes, flipping halfway through, until golden brown and crispy.
6. Serve with lemon wedges.

Nutrition Facts (per serving): Calories: 210 kcal | Protein: 24 g | Carbs: 10 g | Fat: 9 g | Fiber: 1 g | Sugar: 0 g

73. Air Fryer Fish Tacos

□□□Prep time: 10 min | Cook time: 10 min | Servings: 4

Ingredients:

- 1 pound white fish fillets (such as cod or tilapia)
- 1/2 cup breadcrumbs
- 1/4 cup cornmeal
- 1 teaspoon chili powder
- 1 teaspoon garlic powder
- 1 teaspoon cumin
- 2 eggs, beaten
- 8 small corn tortillas
- 1 cup shredded cabbage
- 1/4 cup chopped cilantro
- Lime wedges for serving
- Salt and pepper to taste

Instructions:

1. Preheat air fryer to 200 degrees Celsius.
2. In a shallow bowl, mix breadcrumbs, cornmeal, chili powder, garlic powder, cumin, salt, and pepper.
3. Dip each fish fillet in the beaten eggs, then coat with the breadcrumb mixture.
4. Place the fish fillets in the air fryer basket in a single layer.
5. Cook for 10 minutes, flipping halfway through, until golden brown and crispy.
6. Warm the tortillas in the air fryer for 1-2 minutes.
7. Assemble the tacos by placing the fish fillets in the tortillas and topping with shredded cabbage and chopped cilantro.
8. Serve with lime wedges.

Nutrition Facts (per serving): Calories: 270 kcal | Protein: 22 g | Carbs: 28 g | Fat: 9 g | Fiber: 4 g | Sugar: 1 g

74. Garlic Butter Shrimp Skewers

□□□Prep time: 10 min | Cook time: 8 min | Servings: 4

Ingredients:

- 1 pound large shrimp, peeled and deveined
- 1/4 cup melted butter
- 3 garlic cloves, minced
- 1 tablespoon chopped fresh parsley
- Skewers
- Salt and pepper to taste
- Lemon wedges for serving

Instructions:

1. Preheat air fryer to 200 degrees Celsius.
2. In a bowl, mix melted butter, minced garlic, chopped parsley, salt, and pepper.
3. Thread the shrimp onto skewers.
4. Brush the garlic butter mixture over the shrimp.
5. Place the shrimp skewers in the air fryer basket.
6. Cook for 8 minutes, flipping halfway through, until the shrimp are pink and cooked through.
7. Serve with lemon wedges.

Nutrition Facts (per serving): Calories: 200 kcal | Protein: 23 g | Carbs: 1 g | Fat: 12 g | Fiber: 0 g | Sugar: 0 g

75. Air Fryer Tilapia with Herbs

□□□Prep time: 5 min | Cook time: 10 min | Servings: 4

Ingredients:

- 4 tilapia fillets
- 2 tablespoons olive oil
- 1 teaspoon dried thyme
- 1 teaspoon dried rosemary
- 1 teaspoon garlic powder
- Salt and pepper to taste
- Lemon wedges for serving

Instructions:

1. Preheat air fryer to 200 degrees Celsius.
2. In a small bowl, mix olive oil, dried thyme, dried rosemary, garlic powder, salt, and pepper.
3. Brush the herb mixture over the tilapia fillets.
4. Place the tilapia fillets in the air fryer basket.
5. Cook for 10 minutes, or until the tilapia is cooked through and flakes easily with a fork.
6. Serve with lemon wedges.

Nutrition Facts (per serving): Calories: 180 kcal | Protein: 25 g | Carbs: 1 g | Fat: 8 g | Fiber: 0 g | Sugar: 0 g

76. Blackened Salmon

Prep time: 5 min | Cook time: 12 min | Servings: 4

Ingredients:

- 4 salmon fillets
- 2 tablespoons olive oil
- 1 tablespoon paprika
- 1 teaspoon garlic powder
- 1 teaspoon onion powder
- 1 teaspoon dried oregano
- 1 teaspoon dried thyme
- 1/2 teaspoon cayenne pepper
- Salt and pepper to taste
- Lemon wedges for serving

Instructions:

1. Preheat air fryer to 200 degrees Celsius.
2. In a small bowl, mix paprika, garlic powder, onion powder, dried oregano, dried thyme, cayenne pepper, salt, and pepper.
3. Brush the salmon fillets with olive oil, then coat with the spice mixture.
4. Place the salmon fillets in the air fryer basket.
5. Cook for 12 minutes, or until the salmon is cooked through and flakes easily with a fork.
6. Serve with lemon wedges.

Nutrition Facts (per serving): Calories: 250 kcal | Protein: 23 g | Carbs: 2 g | Fat: 16 g | Fiber: 1 g | Sugar: 0 g

77. Air Fryer Crab Cakes

Prep time: 15 min | Cook time: 10 min | Servings: 4

Ingredients:

- 1 pound crab meat, picked over for shells
- 1/2 cup breadcrumbs
- 1/4 cup mayonnaise
- 1 egg, beaten
- 2 tablespoons chopped fresh parsley
- 1 tablespoon Dijon mustard
- 1 teaspoon Old Bay seasoning
- Cooking spray
- Lemon wedges for serving

Instructions:

1. Preheat air fryer to 200 degrees Celsius.
2. In a large bowl, combine crab meat, breadcrumbs, mayonnaise, beaten egg, chopped parsley, Dijon mustard, and Old Bay seasoning. Mix until well combined.

3. Form the mixture into 8 patties.
4. Spray the air fryer basket with cooking spray and place the crab cakes in a single layer.
5. Cook for 10 minutes, flipping halfway through, until golden brown and crispy.
6. Serve with lemon wedges.

Nutrition Facts (per serving): Calories: 220 kcal | Protein: 20 g | Carbs: 12 g | Fat: 10 g | Fiber: 1 g | Sugar: 1 g

78. Honey Glazed Salmon

⬜⬜⬜Prep time: 5 min | Cook time: 12 min | Servings: 4

Ingredients:
- 4 salmon fillets
- 2 tablespoons honey
- 2 tablespoons soy sauce (low sodium)
- 1 tablespoon olive oil
- 1 garlic clove, minced
- Salt and pepper to taste
- Lemon wedges for serving

Instructions:
1. Preheat air fryer to 200 degrees Celsius.
2. In a small bowl, mix honey, soy sauce, olive oil, minced garlic, salt, and pepper.

3. Brush the mixture over the salmon fillets.
4. Place the salmon fillets in the air fryer basket.
5. Cook for 12 minutes, or until the salmon is cooked through and flakes easily with a fork.
6. Serve with lemon wedges.

Nutrition Facts (per serving): Calories: 250 kcal | Protein: 23 g | Carbs: 10 g | Fat: 14 g | Fiber: 0 g | Sugar: 8 g

79. Air Fryer Cod Fillets

Prep time: 5 min | Cook time: 10 min | Servings: 4

Ingredients:
- 4 cod fillets
- 2 tablespoons olive oil
- 1 teaspoon garlic powder
- 1 teaspoon paprika
- Salt and pepper to taste
- Lemon wedges for serving

Instructions:
1. Preheat air fryer to 200 degrees Celsius.
2. In a small bowl, mix olive oil, garlic powder, paprika, salt, and pepper.
3. Brush the mixture over the cod fillets.
4. Place the cod fillets in the air fryer basket.
5. Cook for 10 minutes, or until the cod is cooked through and flakes easily with a fork.
6. Serve with lemon wedges.

Nutrition Facts (per serving): Calories: 180 kcal | Protein: 23 g | Carbs: 1 g | Fat: 8 g | Fiber: 0 g | Sugar: 0 g

80. Shrimp and Veggie Stir-Fry

Prep time: 10 min | Cook time: 10 min | Servings: 4

Ingredients:
- 1 pound large shrimp, peeled and deveined
- 1 cup broccoli florets
- 1 red bell pepper, sliced
- 1 carrot, sliced
- 1/2 cup snap peas
- 2 tablespoons soy sauce (low sodium)
- 1 tablespoon olive oil
- 1 teaspoon garlic powder
- 1 teaspoon ginger powder
- Salt and pepper to taste

Instructions:
1. Preheat air fryer to 200 degrees Celsius.

2. In a large bowl, toss shrimp, broccoli, bell pepper, carrot, and snap peas with olive oil, garlic powder, ginger powder, salt, and pepper.
3. Spread the shrimp and vegetables in the air fryer basket in a single layer.
4. Cook for 10 minutes, shaking the basket halfway through, until the shrimp are pink and the vegetables are tender.
5. Transfer to a serving bowl and toss with soy sauce.
6. Serve warm.

Nutrition Facts (per serving): Calories: 200 kcal | Protein: 24 g | Carbs: 8 g | Fat: 8 g | Fiber: 2 g | Sugar: 2 g

81. Air Fryer Scallops

Prep time: 5 min | Cook time: 10 min | Servings: 4

Ingredients:
- 1 pound scallops
- 2 tablespoons olive oil
- 2 garlic cloves, minced
- 1 tablespoon lemon juice
- Salt and pepper to taste
- Lemon wedges for serving

Instructions:
1. Preheat air fryer to 200 degrees Celsius.
2. In a bowl, toss scallops with olive oil, minced garlic, lemon juice, salt, and pepper.
3. Place the scallops in the air fryer basket in a single layer.
4. Cook for 10 minutes, flipping halfway through, until the scallops are golden brown and cooked through.
5. Serve with lemon wedges.

Nutrition Facts (per serving): Calories: 160 kcal | Protein: 25 g | Carbs: 2 g | Fat: 6 g | Fiber: 0 g | Sugar: 0 g

82. Herb Crusted Tilapia

Prep time: 10 min | Cook time: 10 min | Servings: 4

Ingredients:
- 4 tilapia fillets
- 1/2 cup breadcrumbs
- 1/4 cup grated Parmesan cheese
- 1 teaspoon dried thyme
- 1 teaspoon dried oregano
- 2 eggs, beaten
- Salt and pepper to taste

Instructions:
1. Preheat air fryer to 200 degrees Celsius.

2. In a shallow bowl, mix breadcrumbs, Parmesan cheese, dried thyme, dried oregano, salt, and pepper.
3. Dip each tilapia fillet in the beaten eggs, then coat with the breadcrumb mixture.
4. Place the tilapia fillets in the air fryer basket in a single layer.
5. Cook for 10 minutes, flipping halfway through, until golden brown and crispy.
6. Serve warm.

Nutrition Facts (per serving): Calories: 230 kcal | Protein: 26 g | Carbs: 10 g | Fat: 10 g | Fiber: 1 g | Sugar: 0 g

83. Air Fryer Mahi Mahi

□□□Prep time: 5 min | Cook time: 10 min | Servings: 4

Ingredients:
- 4 mahi mahi fillets
- 2 tablespoons olive oil
- 1 teaspoon garlic powder
- 1 teaspoon paprika
- Salt and pepper to taste
- Lemon wedges for serving

Instructions:
1. Preheat air fryer to 200 degrees Celsius.
2. In a small bowl, mix olive oil, garlic powder, paprika, salt, and pepper.
3. Brush the mixture over the mahi mahi fillets.
4. Place the mahi mahi fillets in the air fryer basket.
5. Cook for 10 minutes, or until the mahi mahi is cooked through and flakes easily with a fork.
6. Serve with lemon wedges.

Nutrition Facts (per serving): Calories: 200 kcal | Protein: 26 g | Carbs: 1 g | Fat: 10 g | Fiber: 0 g | Sugar: 0 g

84. Coconut Shrimp

□□□Prep time: 15 min | Cook time: 10 min | Servings: 4

Ingredients:
- 1 pound large shrimp, peeled and deveined
- 1/2 cup shredded coconut
- 1/2 cup breadcrumbs
- 2 eggs, beaten
- 2 tablespoons coconut flour
- 1 tablespoon olive oil
- Salt and pepper to taste

Instructions:
1. Preheat air fryer to 200 degrees Celsius.
2. In a shallow bowl, mix shredded coconut, breadcrumbs, coconut flour, salt, and pepper.

3. Dip each shrimp in the beaten eggs, then coat with the coconut mixture.
4. Place the shrimp in the air fryer basket in a single layer.
5. Cook for 10 minutes, flipping halfway through, until golden brown and crispy.
6. Serve warm.

Nutrition Facts (per serving): Calories: 250 kcal | Protein: 24 g | Carbs: 12 g | Fat: 10 g | Fiber: 2 g | Sugar: 3 g

85. Air Fryer Fish Sticks

Prep time: 15 min | Cook time: 10 min | Servings: 4

Ingredients:
- 1 pound white fish fillets (such as cod or haddock), cut into sticks
- 1/2 cup breadcrumbs
- 1/4 cup grated Parmesan cheese
- 1 teaspoon garlic powder
- 1 teaspoon paprika
- 2 eggs, beaten
- Salt and pepper to taste

Instructions:
1. Preheat air fryer to 200 degrees Celsius.
2. In a shallow bowl, mix breadcrumbs, Parmesan cheese, garlic powder, paprika, salt, and pepper.
3. Dip each fish stick in the beaten eggs, then coat with the breadcrumb mixture.
4. Place the fish sticks in the air fryer basket in a single layer.
5. Cook for 10 minutes, flipping halfway through, until golden brown and crispy.
6. Serve warm.

Nutrition Facts (per serving): Calories: 220 kcal | Protein: 22 g | Carbs: 12 g | Fat: 10 g | Fiber: 1 g | Sugar: 0 g

86. Lemon Pepper Air Fryer Trout

Prep time: 5 min | Cook time: 12 min | Servings: 4

Ingredients:
- 4 trout fillets
- 2 tablespoons olive oil
- 1 tablespoon lemon juice
- 1 teaspoon lemon pepper seasoning
- Salt to taste
- Lemon wedges for serving

Instructions:
1. Preheat air fryer to 200 degrees Celsius.
2. In a small bowl, mix olive oil, lemon juice, lemon pepper seasoning, and salt.
3. Brush the mixture over the trout fillets.
4. Place the trout fillets in the air fryer basket.

5. Cook for 12 minutes, or until the trout is cooked through and flakes easily with a fork.
6. Serve with lemon wedges.

Nutrition Facts (per serving): Calories: 200 kcal | Protein: 23 g | Carbs: 1 g | Fat: 12 g | Fiber: 0 g | Sugar: 0 g

87. Air Fryer Clam Strips

Prep time: 15 min | Cook time: 10 min | Servings: 4

Ingredients:
- 1 pound clam strips
- 1/2 cup breadcrumbs
- 1/4 cup cornmeal
- 1 teaspoon Old Bay seasoning
- 2 eggs, beaten
- Salt and pepper to taste
- Lemon wedges for serving

Instructions:
1. Preheat air fryer to 200 degrees Celsius.
2. In a shallow bowl, mix breadcrumbs, cornmeal, Old Bay seasoning, salt, and pepper.
3. Dip each clam strip in the beaten eggs, then coat with the breadcrumb mixture.
4. Place the clam strips in the air fryer basket in a single layer.
5. Cook for 10 minutes, flipping halfway through, until golden brown and crispy.
6. Serve with lemon wedges.

Nutrition Facts (per serving): Calories: 200 kcal | Protein: 16 g | Carbs: 18 g | Fat: 8 g | Fiber: 1 g | Sugar: 1 g

88. Cajun Salmon Patties

Prep time: 15 min | Cook time: 10 min | Servings: 4

Ingredients:
- 1 pound salmon, cooked and flaked
- 1/2 cup breadcrumbs
- 1/4 cup chopped green onions
- 1/4 cup mayonnaise
- 1 egg, beaten
- 1 tablespoon Cajun seasoning
- 1 teaspoon garlic powder
- Salt and pepper to taste
- Cooking spray

Instructions:
1. In a large bowl, combine flaked salmon, breadcrumbs, green onions, mayonnaise, beaten egg, Cajun seasoning, garlic powder, salt, and pepper. Mix until well combined.
2. Form the mixture into 8 patties.

3. Preheat air fryer to 200 degrees Celsius.
4. Spray the air fryer basket with cooking spray and place the salmon patties in a single layer.
5. Cook for 10 minutes, flipping halfway through, until golden brown and crispy.
6. Serve warm.

Nutrition Facts (per serving): Calories: 250 kcal | Protein: 20 g | Carbs: 12 g | Fat: 12 g | Fiber: 1 g | Sugar: 1 g

89. Garlic Parmesan Shrimp

Prep time: 10 min | Cook time: 8 min | Servings: 4

Ingredients:
- 1 pound large shrimp, peeled and deveined
- 1/4 cup grated Parmesan cheese
- 2 tablespoons olive oil
- 2 garlic cloves, minced
- 1 tablespoon chopped fresh parsley
- Salt and pepper to taste
- Lemon wedges for serving

Instructions:
1. Preheat air fryer to 200 degrees Celsius.
2. In a bowl, toss shrimp with olive oil, minced garlic, Parmesan cheese, chopped parsley, salt, and pepper.
3. Place the shrimp in the air fryer basket in a single layer.
4. Cook for 8 minutes, flipping halfway through, until the shrimp are pink and cooked through.
5. Serve with lemon wedges.

Nutrition Facts (per serving): Calories: 200 kcal | Protein: 24 g | Carbs: 2 g | Fat: 10 g | Fiber: 0 g | Sugar: 0 g

90. Air Fryer Halibut Steaks

Prep time: 5 min | Cook time: 10 min | Servings: 4

Ingredients:
- 4 halibut steaks
- 2 tablespoons olive oil
- 1 teaspoon garlic powder
- 1 teaspoon paprika
- Salt and pepper to taste
- Lemon wedges for serving

Instructions:
1. Preheat air fryer to 200 degrees Celsius.
2. In a small bowl, mix olive oil, garlic powder, paprika, salt, and pepper.
3. Brush the mixture over the halibut steaks.
4. Place the halibut steaks in the air fryer basket.

5. Cook for 10 minutes, or until the halibut is cooked through and flakes easily with a fork.
6. Serve with lemon wedges.

Nutrition Facts (per serving): Calories: 220 kcal | Protein: 30 g | Carbs: 1 g | Fat: 10 g | Fiber: 0 g | Sugar: 0 g

91. Spicy Tuna Cakes

Prep time: 10 min | Cook time: 10 min | Servings: 4

Ingredients:

- 2 cans tuna, drained
- 1/2 cup breadcrumbs
- 1/4 cup mayonnaise
- 1 egg, beaten
- 2 tablespoons chopped green onions
- 1 tablespoon Sriracha sauce
- 1 teaspoon garlic powder
- Salt and pepper to taste
- Cooking spray

Instructions:

1. In a large bowl, combine tuna, breadcrumbs, mayonnaise, beaten egg, chopped green onions, Sriracha sauce, garlic powder, salt, and pepper. Mix until well combined.
2. Form the mixture into 8 patties.
3. Preheat air fryer to 200 degrees Celsius.
4. Spray the air fryer basket with cooking spray and place the tuna cakes in a single layer.
5. Cook for 10 minutes, flipping halfway through, until golden brown and crispy.
6. Serve warm.

Nutrition Facts (per serving): Calories: 180 kcal | Protein: 20 g | Carbs: 10 g | Fat: 8 g | Fiber: 1 g | Sugar: 1 g

92. Air Fryer Calamari

Prep time: 15 min | Cook time: 10 min | Servings: 4

Ingredients:

- 1 pound calamari rings
- 1/2 cup flour
- 2 eggs, beaten
- 1/2 cup breadcrumbs
- 1/4 cup grated Parmesan cheese
- 1 teaspoon garlic powder
- 1 teaspoon paprika
- Salt and pepper to taste
- Cooking spray
- Lemon wedges for serving

Instructions:

1. Preheat air fryer to 200 degrees Celsius.
2. In a shallow bowl, mix flour, garlic powder, paprika, salt, and pepper.
3. In another shallow bowl, mix breadcrumbs and Parmesan cheese.
4. Dip each calamari ring in the flour mixture, then in the beaten eggs, and finally in the breadcrumb mixture.
5. Spray the air fryer basket with cooking spray and place the calamari rings in a single layer.
6. Cook for 10 minutes, flipping halfway through, until golden brown and crispy.
7. Serve with lemon wedges.

Nutrition Facts (per serving): Calories: 200 kcal | Protein: 18 g | Carbs: 15 g | Fat: 8 g | Fiber: 1 g | Sugar: 1 g

93. Honey Mustard Salmon

Prep time: 5 min | Cook time: 12 min | Servings: 4

Ingredients:

- 4 salmon fillets
- 2 tablespoons honey
- 2 tablespoons Dijon mustard
- 1 tablespoon olive oil
- Salt and pepper to taste
- Lemon wedges for serving

Instructions:

1. Preheat air fryer to 200 degrees Celsius.
2. In a small bowl, mix honey, Dijon mustard, olive oil, salt, and pepper.
3. Brush the mixture over the salmon fillets.
4. Place the salmon fillets in the air fryer basket.
5. Cook for 12 minutes, or until the salmon is cooked through and flakes easily with a fork.
6. Serve with lemon wedges.

Nutrition Facts (per serving): Calories: 250 kcal | Protein: 23 g | Carbs: 10 g | Fat: 14 g | Fiber: 0 g | Sugar: 8 g

94. Air Fryer Lobster Tails

Prep time: 5 min | Cook time: 10 min | Servings: 4

Ingredients:

- 4 lobster tails
- 1/4 cup melted butter
- 2 garlic cloves, minced
- 1 tablespoon lemon juice
- Salt and pepper to taste
- Lemon wedges for serving

Instructions:

1. Preheat air fryer to 200 degrees Celsius.
2. In a small bowl, mix melted butter, minced garlic, lemon juice, salt, and pepper.
3. Brush the mixture over the lobster tails.
4. Place the lobster tails in the air fryer basket.
5. Cook for 10 minutes, or until the lobster meat is opaque and cooked through.
6. Serve with lemon wedges.

Nutrition Facts (per serving): Calories: 200 kcal | Protein: 20 g | Carbs: 1 g | Fat: 12 g | Fiber: 0 g | Sugar: 0 g

95. Baked Cod with Vegetables

Prep time: 10 min | Cook time: 15 min | Servings: 4

Ingredients:

- 4 cod fillets
- 1 zucchini, sliced
- 1 red bell pepper, sliced
- 1 yellow bell pepper, sliced
- 1 red onion, sliced
- 2 tablespoons olive oil
- 1 teaspoon garlic powder
- 1 teaspoon dried oregano
- Salt and pepper to taste
- Lemon wedges for serving

Instructions:

1. Preheat air fryer to 200 degrees Celsius.
2. In a large bowl, toss zucchini, bell peppers, and onion with olive oil, garlic powder, dried oregano, salt, and pepper.
3. Spread the vegetables in the air fryer basket in a single layer.
4. Place the cod fillets on top of the vegetables.
5. Cook for 15 minutes, or until the cod is cooked through and flakes easily with a fork, and the vegetables are tender.
6. Serve with lemon wedges.

Nutrition Facts (per serving): Calories: 200 kcal | Protein: 23 g | Carbs: 10 g | Fat: 8 g | Fiber: 2 g | Sugar: 3 g

96. Air Fryer Sea Bass

Prep time: 5 min | Cook time: 10 min | Servings: 4

Ingredients:

- 4 sea bass fillets
- 2 tablespoons olive oil
- 1 teaspoon garlic powder
- 1 teaspoon paprika

- Salt and pepper to taste
- Lemon wedges for serving

Instructions:

1. Preheat air fryer to 200 degrees Celsius.
2. In a small bowl, mix olive oil, garlic powder, paprika, salt, and pepper.
3. Brush the mixture over the sea bass fillets.
4. Place the sea bass fillets in the air fryer basket.
5. Cook for 10 minutes, or until the sea bass is cooked through and flakes easily with a fork.
6. Serve with lemon wedges.

Nutrition Facts (per serving): Calories: 220 kcal | Protein: 26 g | Carbs: 1 g | Fat: 12 g | Fiber: 0 g | Sugar: 0 g

97. Chili Lime Shrimp

Prep time: 10 min | Cook time: 8 min | Servings: 4

Ingredients:

- 1 pound large shrimp, peeled and deveined
- 2 tablespoons olive oil
- 1 tablespoon lime juice
- 1 teaspoon chili powder
- 1/2 teaspoon garlic powder
- Salt and pepper to taste
- Lime wedges for serving

Instructions:

1. Preheat air fryer to 200 degrees Celsius.
2. In a bowl, toss shrimp with olive oil, lime juice, chili powder, garlic powder, salt, and pepper.
3. Place the shrimp in the air fryer basket in a single layer.
4. Cook for 8 minutes, flipping halfway through, until the shrimp are pink and cooked through.
5. Serve with lime wedges.

Nutrition Facts (per serving): Calories: 200 kcal | Protein: 24 g | Carbs: 2 g | Fat: 10 g | Fiber: 0 g | Sugar: 0 g

98. Air Fryer Smoked Salmon

Prep time: 5 min | Cook time: 10 min | Servings: 4

Ingredients:

- 4 smoked salmon fillets
- 2 tablespoons olive oil
- 1 teaspoon dill
- 1 teaspoon lemon zest
- Salt and pepper to taste
- Lemon wedges for serving

Instructions:

1. Preheat air fryer to 200 degrees Celsius.
2. In a small bowl, mix olive oil, dill, lemon zest, salt, and pepper.
3. Brush the mixture over the smoked salmon fillets.
4. Place the smoked salmon fillets in the air fryer basket.
5. Cook for 10 minutes, or until the salmon is heated through and slightly crispy on the edges.
6. Serve with lemon wedges.

Nutrition Facts (per serving): Calories: 200 kcal | Protein: 23 g | Carbs: 1 g | Fat: 12 g | Fiber: 0 g | Sugar: 0 g

99. Pesto Crusted Cod

Prep time: 10 min | Cook time: 10 min | Servings: 4

Ingredients:

- 4 cod fillets
- 1/4 cup pesto sauce
- 1/4 cup breadcrumbs
- 1/4 cup grated Parmesan cheese
- 2 tablespoons olive oil
- Salt and pepper to taste
- Lemon wedges for serving

Instructions:

1. Preheat air fryer to 200 degrees Celsius.
2. In a small bowl, mix pesto sauce, breadcrumbs, Parmesan cheese, olive oil, salt, and pepper.
3. Spread the pesto mixture over the cod fillets.
4. Place the cod fillets in the air fryer basket.
5. Cook for 10 minutes, or until the cod is cooked through and flakes easily with a fork.
6. Serve with lemon wedges.

Nutrition Facts (per serving): Calories: 250 kcal | Protein: 23 g | Carbs: 5 g | Fat: 14 g | Fiber: 1 g | Sugar: 0 g

100. Air Fryer Swordfish

Prep time: 5 min | Cook time: 10 min | Servings: 4

Ingredients:

- 4 swordfish steaks
- 2 tablespoons olive oil
- 1 teaspoon garlic powder
- 1 teaspoon paprika
- Salt and pepper to taste
- Lemon wedges for serving

Instructions:

1. Preheat air fryer to 200 degrees Celsius.
2. In a small bowl, mix olive oil, garlic powder, paprika, salt, and pepper.

3. Brush the mixture over the swordfish steaks.
4. Place the swordfish steaks in the air fryer basket.
5. Cook for 10 minutes, or until the swordfish is cooked through and flakes easily with a fork.
6. Serve with lemon wedges.

Nutrition Facts (per serving): Calories: 220 kcal | Protein: 30 g | Carbs: 1 g | Fat: 10 g | Fiber: 0 g | Sugar: 0 g

Meat Recipes

101. Air Fryer Chicken Breast

☐☐☐Prep time: 5 min | Cook time: 15 min | Servings: 4

Ingredients:
- 4 boneless, skinless chicken breasts
- 2 tablespoons olive oil
- 1 teaspoon garlic powder
- 1 teaspoon paprika
- Salt and pepper to taste

Instructions:
1. Preheat air fryer to 200 degrees Celsius.
2. In a small bowl, mix olive oil, garlic powder, paprika, salt, and pepper.
3. Brush the mixture over the chicken breasts.
4. Place the chicken breasts in the air fryer basket.
5. Cook for 15 minutes, flipping halfway through, until the chicken is cooked through and juices run clear.
6. Serve warm.

Nutrition Facts (per serving): Calories: 220 kcal | Protein: 26 g | Carbs: 1 g | Fat: 12 g | Fiber: 0 g | Sugar: 0 g

102. Garlic Herb Pork Chops

☐☐☐Prep time: 10 min | Cook time: 15 min | Servings: 4

Ingredients:
- 4 pork chops
- 2 tablespoons olive oil
- 2 garlic cloves, minced
- 1 teaspoon dried rosemary
- 1 teaspoon dried thyme
- Salt and pepper to taste

Instructions:
1. Preheat air fryer to 200 degrees Celsius.
2. In a small bowl, mix olive oil, minced garlic, dried rosemary, dried thyme, salt, and pepper.

3. Brush the mixture over the pork chops.
4. Place the pork chops in the air fryer basket.
5. Cook for 15 minutes, flipping halfway through, until the pork is cooked through and juices run clear.
6. Serve warm.

Nutrition Facts (per serving): Calories: 250 kcal | Protein: 26 g | Carbs: 1 g | Fat: 15 g | Fiber: 0 g | Sugar: 0 g

103. Air Fryer Meatballs

☐☐☐Prep time: 15 min | Cook time: 10 min | Servings: 4

Ingredients:
- 1 pound ground beef
- 1/2 cup breadcrumbs
- 1/4 cup grated Parmesan cheese
- 1 egg, beaten
- 2 garlic cloves, minced
- 1 teaspoon dried oregano
- Salt and pepper to taste

Instructions:

1. In a large bowl, combine ground beef, breadcrumbs, Parmesan cheese, beaten egg, minced garlic, dried oregano, salt, and pepper. Mix until well combined.
2. Form the mixture into 16 meatballs.
3. Preheat air fryer to 200 degrees Celsius.
4. Place the meatballs in the air fryer basket in a single layer.
5. Cook for 10 minutes, flipping halfway through, until golden brown and cooked through.
6. Serve warm.

Nutrition Facts (per serving): Calories: 220 kcal | Protein: 20 g | Carbs: 8 g | Fat: 12 g | Fiber: 1 g | Sugar: 1 g

104. Lemon Pepper Chicken Wings

⬜⬜⬜Prep time: 10 min | Cook time: 25 min | Servings: 4

Ingredients:

- 2 pounds chicken wings
- 2 tablespoons olive oil
- 1 tablespoon lemon pepper seasoning
- Salt to taste

Instructions:

1. Preheat air fryer to 200 degrees Celsius.
2. In a large bowl, toss chicken wings with olive oil, lemon pepper seasoning, and salt.
3. Place the chicken wings in the air fryer basket in a single layer.
4. Cook for 25 minutes, flipping halfway through, until golden brown and crispy.
5. Serve warm.

Nutrition Facts (per serving): Calories: 350 kcal | Protein: 25 g | Carbs: 1 g | Fat: 28 g | Fiber: 0 g | Sugar: 0 g

105. Air Fryer Beef Kabobs

⬜⬜⬜Prep time: 15 min | Cook time: 10 min | Servings: 4

Ingredients:

- 1 pound beef sirloin, cut into cubes
- 1 red bell pepper, cut into squares
- 1 yellow bell pepper, cut into squares
- 1 red onion, cut into squares
- 2 tablespoons olive oil
- 1 tablespoon soy sauce (low sodium)
- 1 teaspoon garlic powder
- 1 teaspoon smoked paprika
- Salt and pepper to taste
- Skewers

Instructions:

1. In a large bowl, mix olive oil, soy sauce, garlic powder, smoked paprika, salt, and pepper.
2. Add beef cubes, bell peppers, and onion to the bowl and toss to coat.
3. Thread beef and vegetables onto skewers.
4. Preheat air fryer to 200 degrees Celsius.
5. Place the skewers in the air fryer basket in a single layer.
6. Cook for 10 minutes, flipping halfway through, until the beef is cooked to your desired doneness.
7. Serve warm.

Nutrition Facts (per serving): Calories: 300 kcal | Protein: 25 g | Carbs: 6 g | Fat: 20 g | Fiber: 2 g | Sugar: 2 g

106. BBQ Chicken Thighs

Prep time: 10 min | Cook time: 20 min | Servings: 4

Ingredients:
- 8 chicken thighs
- 1/2 cup BBQ sauce
- 2 tablespoons olive oil
- 1 teaspoon garlic powder
- Salt and pepper to taste

Instructions:
1. Preheat air fryer to 200 degrees Celsius.
2. In a large bowl, toss chicken thighs with olive oil, garlic powder, salt, and pepper.
3. Place the chicken thighs in the air fryer basket in a single layer.
4. Cook for 15 minutes, flipping halfway through.
5. Brush BBQ sauce over the chicken thighs and cook for an additional 5 minutes.
6. Serve warm.

Nutrition Facts (per serving): Calories: 320 kcal | Protein: 24 g | Carbs: 10 g | Fat: 20 g | Fiber: 0 g | Sugar: 8 g

107. Air Fryer Turkey Burgers

Prep time: 10 min | Cook time: 15 min | Servings: 4

Ingredients:
- 1 pound ground turkey
- 1/4 cup breadcrumbs
- 1 egg, beaten
- 1/4 cup finely chopped onions
- 1 teaspoon garlic powder
- 1 teaspoon paprika
- Salt and pepper to taste
- Whole grain buns for serving

Instructions:

1. In a large bowl, combine ground turkey, breadcrumbs, beaten egg, chopped onions, garlic powder, paprika, salt, and pepper. Mix until well combined.
2. Form the mixture into 4 patties.
3. Preheat air fryer to 200 degrees Celsius.
4. Place the turkey patties in the air fryer basket in a single layer.
5. Cook for 15 minutes, flipping halfway through, until the internal temperature reaches 74 degrees Celsius.
6. Serve warm on whole grain buns with your favorite toppings.

Nutrition Facts (per serving): Calories: 250 kcal | Protein: 25 g | Carbs: 10 g | Fat: 12 g | Fiber: 1 g | Sugar: 1 g

108. Herb-Crusted Pork Tenderloin

□□□Prep time: 10 min | Cook time: 20 min | Servings: 4

Ingredients:
- 1 pork tenderloin
- 2 tablespoons olive oil
- 1 teaspoon dried rosemary
- 1 teaspoon dried thyme
- 1 teaspoon garlic powder
- Salt and pepper to taste

Instructions:
1. Preheat air fryer to 200 degrees Celsius.
2. In a small bowl, mix olive oil, dried rosemary, dried thyme, garlic powder, salt, and pepper.
3. Rub the mixture over the pork tenderloin.
4. Place the pork tenderloin in the air fryer basket.
5. Cook for 20 minutes, flipping halfway through, until the internal temperature reaches 63 degrees Celsius.
6. Let rest for 5 minutes before slicing and serving.

Nutrition Facts (per serving): Calories: 250 kcal | Protein: 30 g | Carbs: 1 g | Fat: 14 g | Fiber: 0 g | Sugar: 0 g

109. Air Fryer Lamb Chops

□□□Prep time: 10 min | Cook time: 15 min | Servings: 4

Ingredients:
- 8 lamb chops
- 2 tablespoons olive oil
- 2 garlic cloves, minced
- 1 teaspoon dried rosemary
- 1 teaspoon dried thyme
- Salt and pepper to taste

Instructions:

1. Preheat air fryer to 200 degrees Celsius.
2. In a small bowl, mix olive oil, minced garlic, dried rosemary, dried thyme, salt, and pepper.
3. Brush the mixture over the lamb chops.
4. Place the lamb chops in the air fryer basket in a single layer.
5. Cook for 15 minutes, flipping halfway through, until the internal temperature reaches 63 degrees Celsius.
6. Let rest for 5 minutes before serving.

Nutrition Facts (per serving): Calories: 300 kcal | Protein: 25 g | Carbs: 1 g | Fat: 22 g | Fiber: 0 g | Sugar: 0 g

110. Cajun Chicken Drumsticks

Prep time: 10 min | Cook time: 25 min | Servings: 4

Ingredients:
- 8 chicken drumsticks
- 2 tablespoons olive oil
- 1 tablespoon Cajun seasoning
- Salt to taste

Instructions:
1. Preheat air fryer to 200 degrees Celsius.
2. In a large bowl, toss chicken drumsticks with olive oil, Cajun seasoning, and salt.
3. Place the chicken drumsticks in the air fryer basket in a single layer.
4. Cook for 25 minutes, flipping halfway through, until golden brown and crispy.
5. Serve warm.

Nutrition Facts (per serving): Calories: 320 kcal | Protein: 26 g | Carbs: 1 g | Fat: 22 g | Fiber: 0 g | Sugar: 0 g

111. Air Fryer Steak Bites

Prep time: 10 min | Cook time: 10 min | Servings: 4

Ingredients:
- 1 pound steak, cut into bite-sized pieces
- 2 tablespoons olive oil
- 1 teaspoon garlic powder
- 1 teaspoon onion powder
- 1 teaspoon smoked paprika
- Salt and pepper to taste

Instructions:
1. Preheat air fryer to 200 degrees Celsius.
2. In a large bowl, toss steak pieces with olive oil, garlic powder, onion powder, smoked paprika, salt, and pepper.
3. Place the steak bites in the air fryer basket in a single layer.

4. Cook for 10 minutes, shaking the basket halfway through, until the steak bites are cooked to your desired doneness.
5. Serve warm.

Nutrition Facts (per serving): Calories: 250 kcal | Protein: 26 g | Carbs: 1 g | Fat: 16 g | Fiber: 0 g | Sugar: 0 g

112. Teriyaki Chicken

□□□Prep time: 10 min | Cook time: 15 min | Servings: 4

Ingredients:
- 4 boneless, skinless chicken breasts
- 1/4 cup soy sauce (low sodium)
- 2 tablespoons honey
- 1 tablespoon rice vinegar
- 1 garlic clove, minced
- 1 teaspoon ginger powder
- 2 tablespoons olive oil
- Salt and pepper to taste

Instructions:
1. In a small bowl, mix soy sauce, honey, rice vinegar, minced garlic, ginger powder, salt, and pepper.
2. Place chicken breasts in a resealable bag and pour the marinade over them. Seal the bag and marinate in the refrigerator for at least 30 minutes.
3. Preheat air fryer to 200 degrees Celsius.
4. Remove the chicken breasts from the marinade and discard the marinade.
5. Brush the chicken breasts with olive oil.
6. Place the chicken breasts in the air fryer basket in a single layer.
7. Cook for 15 minutes, flipping halfway through, until the chicken is cooked through and juices run clear.
8. Serve warm.

Nutrition Facts (per serving): Calories: 250 kcal | Protein: 26 g | Carbs: 10 g | Fat: 10 g | Fiber: 0 g | Sugar: 8 g

113. Air Fryer Pork Schnitzel

□□□Prep time: 10 min | Cook time: 10 min | Servings: 4

Ingredients:
- 4 pork cutlets
- 1/2 cup breadcrumbs
- 1/4 cup grated Parmesan cheese
- 2 eggs, beaten
- 2 tablespoons flour
- 2 tablespoons olive oil
- Salt and pepper to taste

Instructions:

1. Preheat air fryer to 200 degrees Celsius.
2. In a shallow bowl, mix breadcrumbs, Parmesan cheese, salt, and pepper.
3. Dip each pork cutlet in the flour, then in the beaten eggs, and finally in the breadcrumb mixture.
4. Brush the breaded cutlets with olive oil.
5. Place the pork cutlets in the air fryer basket in a single layer.
6. Cook for 10 minutes, flipping halfway through, until golden brown and crispy.
7. Serve warm.

Nutrition Facts (per serving): Calories: 280 kcal | Protein: 26 g | Carbs: 10 g | Fat: 14 g | Fiber: 1 g | Sugar: 1 g

114. Greek Chicken Skewers

Prep time: 15 min | Cook time: 10 min | Servings: 4

Ingredients:

- 1 pound chicken breast, cut into cubes
- 1/4 cup olive oil
- 2 tablespoons lemon juice
- 2 garlic cloves, minced
- 1 tablespoon dried oregano
- Salt and pepper to taste
- Skewers

Instructions:

1. In a bowl, mix olive oil, lemon juice, minced garlic, dried oregano, salt, and pepper.
2. Add chicken cubes to the bowl and toss to coat.
3. Thread the chicken onto skewers.
4. Preheat air fryer to 200 degrees Celsius.
5. Place the skewers in the air fryer basket in a single layer.
6. Cook for 10 minutes, flipping halfway through, until the chicken is cooked through and juices run clear. 7
7. Serve warm with a side of tzatziki sauce.

Nutrition Facts (per serving): Calories: 220 kcal | Protein: 26 g | Carbs: 2 g | Fat: 12 g | Fiber: 0

115. BBQ Ribs

Prep time: 15 min | Cook time: 30 min | Servings: 4

Ingredients:

- 2 pounds pork ribs
- 1/2 cup BBQ sauce
- 2 tablespoons olive oil
- 1 teaspoon garlic powder
- Salt and pepper to taste

Instructions:

1. Preheat air fryer to 200 degrees Celsius.
2. In a large bowl, toss pork ribs with olive oil, garlic powder, salt, and pepper.
3. Place the ribs in the air fryer basket in a single layer.
4. Cook for 20 minutes, flipping halfway through.
5. Brush BBQ sauce over the ribs and cook for an additional 10 minutes.
6. Serve warm.

Nutrition Facts (per serving): Calories: 400 kcal | Protein: 25 g | Carbs: 10 g | Fat: 30 g | Fiber: 0 g Sugar: 8 g

116. Herb-Crusted Lamb Chops

Prep time: 10 min | Cook time: 15 min | Servings: 4

Ingredients:
- 8 lamb chops
- 2 tablespoons olive oil
- 2 garlic cloves, minced
- 1 teaspoon dried rosemary
- 1 teaspoon dried thyme
- Salt and pepper to taste

Instructions:
1. Preheat air fryer to 200 degrees Celsius.
2. In a small bowl, mix olive oil, minced garlic, dried rosemary, dried thyme, salt, and pepper.
3. Brush the mixture over the lamb chops.
4. Place the lamb chops in the air fryer basket in a single layer.
5. Cook for 15 minutes, flipping halfway through, until the internal temperature reaches 63 degrees Celsius.
6. Let rest for 5 minutes before serving.

Nutrition Facts (per serving): Calories: 300 kcal | Protein: 25 g | Carbs: 1 g | Fat: 22 g | Fiber: 0 g Sugar: 0 g

117. Air Fryer Meatloaf

Prep time: 15 min | Cook time: 25 min | Servings: 4

Ingredients:
- 1 pound ground beef
- 1/2 cup breadcrumbs
- 1/4 cup grated Parmesan cheese
- 1 egg, beaten
- 1/2 cup ketchup, divided
- 2 garlic cloves, minced
- 1 teaspoon dried oregano
- Salt and pepper to taste

Instructions:

1. In a large bowl, combine ground beef, breadcrumbs, Parmesan cheese, beaten egg, 1/4 cup ketchup, minced garlic, dried oregano, salt, and pepper. Mix until well combined.
2. Form the mixture into a loaf.
3. Preheat air fryer to 200 degrees Celsius.
4. Place the meatloaf in the air fryer basket.
5. Cook for 20 minutes.
6. Brush the remaining 1/4 cup ketchup over the meatloaf and cook for an additional 5 minutes.
7. Let rest for 5 minutes before slicing and serving.

Nutrition Facts (per serving): Calories: 320 kcal | Protein: 24 g | Carbs: 12 g | Fat: 20 g | Fiber: 1 g | Sugar: 6 g

118. Spicy Italian Sausage

Prep time: 5 min | Cook time: 12 min | Servings: 4

Ingredients:
- 4 spicy Italian sausages
- 1 tablespoon olive oil

Instructions:
1. Preheat air fryer to 200 degrees Celsius.
2. Brush sausages with olive oil.
3. Place the sausages in the air fryer basket in a single layer.
4. Cook for 12 minutes, flipping halfway through, until golden brown and cooked through.
5. Serve warm.

Nutrition Facts (per serving): Calories: 300 kcal | Protein: 16 g | Carbs: 2 g | Fat: 26 g | Fiber: 0 g | Sugar: 1 g

119. Honey Mustard Pork Chops

Prep time: 10 min | Cook time: 15 min | Servings: 4

Ingredients:
- 4 pork chops
- 2 tablespoons honey
- 2 tablespoons Dijon mustard
- 1 tablespoon olive oil
- Salt and pepper to taste

Instructions:
1. Preheat air fryer to 200 degrees Celsius.
2. In a small bowl, mix honey, Dijon mustard, olive oil, salt, and pepper.
3. Brush the mixture over the pork chops.
4. Place the pork chops in the air fryer basket in a single layer.
5. Cook for 15 minutes, flipping halfway through, until the pork is cooked through and juices run clear.
6. Serve warm.

Nutrition Facts (per serving): Calories: 250 kcal | Protein: 26 g | Carbs: 10 g | Fat: 12 g | Fiber: 0 g | Sugar: 8 g

120. Air Fryer Chicken Parmesan

☐☐☐Prep time: 15 min | Cook time: 15 min | Servings: 4

Ingredients:

- 4 boneless, skinless chicken breasts
- 1/2 cup breadcrumbs
- 1/4 cup grated Parmesan cheese
- 2 eggs, beaten
- 1 cup marinara sauce
- 1 cup shredded mozzarella cheese
- 2 tablespoons olive oil
- Salt and pepper to taste

Instructions:

1. Preheat air fryer to 200 degrees Celsius.
2. In a shallow bowl, mix breadcrumbs, Parmesan cheese, salt, and pepper.
3. Dip each chicken breast in the beaten eggs, then coat with the breadcrumb mixture.
4. Brush the breaded chicken breasts with olive oil.
5. Place the chicken breasts in the air fryer basket in a single layer.
6. Cook for 10 minutes, flipping halfway through.
7. Top each chicken breast with marinara sauce and shredded mozzarella cheese.
8. Cook for an additional 5 minutes, until the cheese is melted and bubbly.
9. Serve warm.

Nutrition Facts (per serving): Calories: 350 kcal | Protein: 36 g | Carbs: 12 g | Fat: 18 g | Fiber: 1 g | Sugar: 5 g

121. Air Fryer Turkey Meatballs

☐☐☐Prep time: 15 min | Cook time: 10 min | Servings: 4

Ingredients:

- 1 pound ground turkey
- 1/2 cup breadcrumbs
- 1/4 cup grated Parmesan cheese
- 1 egg, beaten
- 2 garlic cloves, minced
- 1 teaspoon dried oregano
- Salt and pepper to taste

Instructions:

1. In a large bowl, combine ground turkey, breadcrumbs, Parmesan cheese, beaten egg, minced garlic, dried oregano, salt, and pepper. Mix until well combined.
2. Form the mixture into 16 meatballs.

3. Preheat air fryer to 200 degrees Celsius.
4. Place the meatballs in the air fryer basket in a single layer.
5. Cook for 10 minutes, flipping halfway through, until golden brown and cooked through.
6. Serve warm.

Nutrition Facts (per serving): Calories: 220 kcal | Protein: 20 g | Carbs: 8 g | Fat: 12 g | Fiber: 1 g | Sugar: 1 g

122. BBQ Chicken Wings

␣␣␣Prep time: 10 min | Cook time: 25 min | Servings: 4

Ingredients:
- 2 pounds chicken wings
- 2 tablespoons olive oil
- 1/2 cup BBQ sauce
- Salt and pepper to taste

Instructions:
1. Preheat air fryer to 200 degrees Celsius.
2. In a large bowl, toss chicken wings with olive oil, salt, and pepper.
3. Place the chicken wings in the air fryer basket in a single layer.
4. Cook for 20 minutes, flipping halfway through.
5. Brush BBQ sauce over the chicken wings and cook for an additional 5 minutes.
6. Serve warm.

Nutrition Facts (per serving): Calories: 350 kcal | Protein: 25 g | Carbs: 10 g | Fat: 26 g | Fiber: 0 g | Sugar: 8 g

123. Herb-Marinated Lamb Chops

␣␣␣Prep time: 10 min | Cook time: 15 min | Servings: 4

Ingredients:
- 8 lamb chops
- 2 tablespoons olive oil
- 2 garlic cloves, minced
- 1 teaspoon dried rosemary
- 1 teaspoon dried thyme
- 1 tablespoon lemon juice
- Salt and pepper to taste

Instructions:
1. In a bowl, mix olive oil, minced garlic, dried rosemary, dried thyme, lemon juice, salt, and pepper.
2. Brush the mixture over the lamb chops and let marinate for at least 30 minutes.
3. Preheat air fryer to 200 degrees Celsius.
4. Place the lamb chops in the air fryer basket in a single layer.
5. Cook for 15 minutes, flipping halfway through, until the internal temperature reaches 63 degrees Celsius.

6. Let rest for 5 minutes before serving.

Nutrition Facts (per serving): Calories: 300 kcal | Protein: 25 g | Carbs: 1 g | Fat: 22 g | Fiber: 0 g
Sugar: 0 g

124. Sweet and Spicy Chicken Thighs

☐☐☐Prep time: 10 min | Cook time: 20 min | Servings: 4

Ingredients:
- 8 chicken thighs
- 2 tablespoons olive oil
- 2 tablespoons honey
- 1 tablespoon Sriracha sauce
- 1 teaspoon garlic powder
- Salt and pepper to taste

Instructions:
1. Preheat air fryer to 200 degrees Celsius.
2. In a bowl, mix olive oil, honey, Sriracha sauce, garlic powder, salt, and pepper.
3. Toss the chicken thighs in the mixture.
4. Place the chicken thighs in the air fryer basket in a single layer.
5. Cook for 20 minutes, flipping halfway through, until the chicken is cooked through and juices run clear.
6. Serve warm.

Nutrition Facts (per serving): Calories: 320 kcal | Protein: 24 g | Carbs: 10 g | Fat: 20 g | Fiber: 0 g
Sugar: 8 g

125. Air Fryer Bacon-Wrapped Chicken

Prep time: 10 min | Cook time: 20 min | Servings: 4

Ingredients:

- 4 boneless, skinless chicken breasts
- 8 slices bacon
- 2 tablespoons olive oil
- 1 teaspoon garlic powder
- 1 teaspoon paprika
- Salt and pepper to taste

Instructions:

1. Preheat air fryer to 200 degrees Celsius.
2. In a small bowl, mix olive oil, garlic powder, paprika, salt, and pepper.
3. Brush the chicken breasts with the olive oil mixture.
4. Wrap each chicken breast with 2 slices of bacon.
5. Place the bacon-wrapped chicken breasts in the air fryer basket in a single layer.
6. Cook for 20 minutes, flipping halfway through, until the bacon is crispy and the chicken is cooked through.
7. Serve warm.

Nutrition Facts (per serving): Calories: 400 kcal | Protein: 36 g | Carbs: 2 g | Fat: 26 g | Fiber: 0 g | Sugar: 0 g

Vegan Recipes

126. Air Fryer Tofu Stir-Fry

Prep time: 10 min | Cook time: 15 min | Servings: 4

Ingredients:

- 1 block firm tofu, pressed and cubed
- 1 cup broccoli florets
- 1 red bell pepper, sliced
- 1 yellow bell pepper, sliced
- 1/2 cup snap peas
- 2 tablespoons soy sauce (low sodium)
- 1 tablespoon olive oil
- 1 teaspoon garlic powder
- 1 teaspoon ginger powder
- Salt and pepper to taste

Instructions:

1. Preheat air fryer to 200 degrees Celsius.
2. In a bowl, toss tofu cubes with olive oil, garlic powder, ginger powder, salt, and pepper.
3. Place tofu in the air fryer basket in a single layer. Cook for 10 minutes, shaking the basket halfway through.

4. In a separate bowl, toss broccoli, bell peppers, and snap peas with soy sauce.
5. Add vegetables to the air fryer with the tofu and cook for an additional 5 minutes until vegetables are tender.
6. Serve warm over rice or noodles.

Nutrition Facts (per serving): Calories: 180 kcal | Protein: 10 g | Carbs: 15 g | Fat: 8 g | Fiber: 4 g | Sugar: 5 g

127. Crispy Chickpea Salad

Prep time: 10 min | Cook time: 15 min | Servings: 4

Ingredients:
- 1 can chickpeas, rinsed and drained
- 1 tablespoon olive oil
- 1 teaspoon smoked paprika
- 1/2 teaspoon garlic powder
- Salt and pepper to taste
- 4 cups mixed salad greens
- 1 cucumber, sliced
- 1 cup cherry tomatoes, halved
- 1/4 cup red onion, thinly sliced
- 1/4 cup vinaigrette dressing

Instructions:
1. Preheat air fryer to 200 degrees Celsius.
2. In a bowl, toss chickpeas with olive oil, smoked paprika, garlic powder, salt, and pepper.
3. Place chickpeas in the air fryer basket in a single layer. Cook for 15 minutes, shaking the basket halfway through until crispy.
4. In a large salad bowl, combine salad greens, cucumber, cherry tomatoes, and red onion.
5. Top salad with crispy chickpeas and drizzle with vinaigrette dressing. Serve immediately.

Nutrition Facts (per serving): Calories: 200 kcal | Protein: 6 g | Carbs: 25 g | Fat: 10 g | Fiber: 7 g | Sugar: 5 g

128. Air Fryer Stuffed Bell Peppers

Prep time: 15 min | Cook time: 20 min | Servings: 4

Ingredients:
- 4 bell peppers, tops removed and seeded
- 1 cup cooked quinoa
- 1 can black beans, rinsed and drained
- 1 cup corn kernels
- 1/2 cup diced tomatoes
- 1/4 cup chopped green onions
- 1 tablespoon taco seasoning
- 1 tablespoon olive oil

- Salt and pepper to taste

Instructions:

1. Preheat air fryer to 180 degrees Celsius.
2. In a large bowl, mix cooked quinoa, black beans, corn, diced tomatoes, green onions, taco seasoning, olive oil, salt, and pepper.
3. Stuff the bell peppers with the quinoa mixture.
4. Place the stuffed peppers in the air fryer basket.
5. Cook for 20 minutes, until the peppers are tender and the filling is heated through.
6. Serve warm.

Nutrition Facts (per serving): Calories: 220 kcal | Protein: 8 g | Carbs: 38 g | Fat: 5 g | Fiber: 10 g | Sugar: 10 g

129. Spicy Tempeh Tacos

Prep time: 10 min | Cook time: 15 min | Servings: 4

Ingredients:

- 1 block tempeh, crumbled
- 2 tablespoons olive oil
- 1 tablespoon soy sauce (low sodium)
- 1 tablespoon hot sauce
- 1 teaspoon chili powder
- 1 teaspoon cumin
- 8 small corn tortillas
- 1 cup shredded lettuce
- 1/2 cup diced tomatoes
- 1/4 cup diced red onion
- 1/4 cup chopped cilantro
- Lime wedges for serving

Instructions:

1. Preheat air fryer to 200 degrees Celsius.
2. In a bowl, toss crumbled tempeh with olive oil, soy sauce, hot sauce, chili powder, and cumin.
3. Place tempeh in the air fryer basket in a single layer. Cook for 15 minutes, shaking the basket halfway through until crispy.
4. Warm tortillas in the air fryer for 1-2 minutes.
5. Assemble tacos by filling each tortilla with tempeh, lettuce, tomatoes, red onion, and cilantro.
6. Serve with lime wedges.

Nutrition Facts (per serving): Calories: 250 kcal | Protein: 10 g | Carbs: 30 g | Fat: 10 g | Fiber: 6 g | Sugar: 3 g

130. Air Fryer Cauliflower Steaks

Prep time: 10 min | Cook time: 20 min | Servings: 4

Ingredients:

- 1 large head of cauliflower, sliced into 1-inch thick steaks
- 2 tablespoons olive oil
- 1 teaspoon garlic powder
- 1 teaspoon smoked paprika
- Salt and pepper to taste
- 1 tablespoon chopped parsley (for garnish)
- Lemon wedges for serving

Instructions:

1. Preheat air fryer to 200 degrees Celsius.
2. In a bowl, mix olive oil, garlic powder, smoked paprika, salt, and pepper.
3. Brush the mixture over both sides of the cauliflower steaks.
4. Place the cauliflower steaks in the air fryer basket in a single layer.
5. Cook for 20 minutes, flipping halfway through, until golden brown and tender.
6. Garnish with chopped parsley and serve with lemon wedges.

Nutrition Facts (per serving): Calories: 100 kcal | Protein: 3 g | Carbs: 10 g | Fat: 6 g | Fiber: 4 g | Sugar: 3 g

Dessert

131. Air Fryer Apple Chips

Prep time: 10 min | Cook time: 15 min | Servings: 4

Ingredients:

- 2 large apples, thinly sliced
- 1 teaspoon ground cinnamon
- 1 tablespoon sugar (optional)

Instructions:

1. Preheat air fryer to 160 degrees Celsius.
2. In a large bowl, toss apple slices with ground cinnamon and sugar if using.
3. Place apple slices in the air fryer basket in a single layer.
4. Cook for 15 minutes, flipping halfway through, until crispy.
5. Serve warm or at room temperature.

Nutrition Facts (per serving): Calories: 60 kcal | Protein: 0 g | Carbs: 16 g | Fat: 0 g | Fiber: 3 g | Sugar: 12 g

132. Baked Cinnamon Pears

Prep time: 10 min | Cook time: 20 min | Servings: 4

Ingredients:

- 4 ripe pears, halved and cored
- 2 tablespoons honey

- 1 teaspoon ground cinnamon
- 1/4 teaspoon ground nutmeg
- 1/4 cup chopped walnuts (optional)

Instructions:

1. Preheat air fryer to 180 degrees Celsius.
2. In a small bowl, mix honey, ground cinnamon, and ground nutmeg.
3. Brush the pear halves with the honey mixture and sprinkle with chopped walnuts if using.
4. Place pears in the air fryer basket in a single layer.
5. Cook for 20 minutes until tender and caramelized.
6. Serve warm.

Nutrition Facts (per serving): Calories: 150 kcal | Protein: 1 g | Carbs: 34 g | Fat: 2 g | Fiber: 6 g | Sugar: 22 g

133. Chocolate Avocado Brownies

Prep time: 10 min | Cook time: 15 min | Servings: 4

Ingredients:

- 1 ripe avocado, mashed
- 1/2 cup flour
- 1/2 cup sugar
- 1/4 cup cocoa powder
- 1/4 cup melted coconut oil
- 2 eggs
- 1 teaspoon vanilla extract
- 1/4 teaspoon baking powder
- 1/4 teaspoon salt

Instructions:

1. Preheat air fryer to 180 degrees Celsius.
2. In a large bowl, mix mashed avocado, flour, sugar, cocoa powder, melted coconut oil, eggs, vanilla extract, baking powder, and salt until well combined.
3. Pour the batter into a greased air fryer-safe baking dish.
4. Cook for 15 minutes, or until a toothpick inserted into the center comes out clean.
5. Let cool slightly before serving.

Nutrition Facts (per serving): Calories: 250 kcal | Protein: 3 g | Carbs: 35 g | Fat: 12 g | Fiber: 2 g | Sugar: 25 g

134. Air Fryer Banana Bread

Prep time: 10 min | Cook time: 25 min | Servings: 4

Ingredients:

- 2 ripe bananas, mashed
- 1 cup flour
- 1/2 cup sugar

- 1/4 cup melted coconut oil
- 1 teaspoon baking powder
- 1 teaspoon vanilla extract
- 1/2 teaspoon ground cinnamon
- 1/4 teaspoon salt

Instructions:

1. Preheat air fryer to 160 degrees Celsius.
2. In a large bowl, mix mashed bananas, flour, sugar, melted coconut oil, baking powder, vanilla extract, ground cinnamon, and salt until well combined.
3. Pour the batter into a greased air fryer-safe baking dish.
4. Cook for 25 minutes, or until a toothpick inserted into the center comes out clean.
5. Let cool slightly before serving.

Nutrition Facts (per serving): Calories: 210 kcal | Protein: 2 g | Carbs: 36 g | Fat: 7 g | Fiber: 2 g | Sugar: 18 g

135. Blueberry Crumble

Prep time: 10 min | Cook time: 20 min | Servings: 4

Ingredients:

- 2 cups fresh blueberries
- 1/4 cup sugar
- 1 tablespoon lemon juice
- 1/2 cup flour
- 1/4 cup oats
- 1/4 cup brown sugar
- 1/4 cup melted butter
- 1/2 teaspoon ground cinnamon
- 1/4 teaspoon salt

Instructions:

1. Preheat air fryer to 180 degrees Celsius.
2. In a bowl, mix blueberries, sugar, and lemon juice. Place in an air fryer-safe baking dish.
3. In a separate bowl, mix flour, oats, brown sugar, melted butter, ground cinnamon, and salt until crumbly.
4. Sprinkle the crumble mixture over the blueberries.
5. Cook for 20 minutes until the topping is golden brown and the blueberries are bubbly.
6. Serve warm.

Nutrition Facts (per serving): Calories: 250 kcal | Protein: 2 g | Carbs: 40 g | Fat: 10 g | Fiber: 4 g | Sugar: 25 g

136. Air Fryer Pumpkin Pie Bites

Prep time: 15 min | Cook time: 10 min | Servings: 4

Ingredients:

- 1 cup pumpkin puree
- 1/4 cup sugar
- 1/2 teaspoon pumpkin pie spice
- 1 egg
- 1/2 teaspoon vanilla extract
- 1 package refrigerated pie crusts
- Cooking spray

Instructions:

1. Preheat air fryer to 180 degrees Celsius.
2. In a bowl, mix pumpkin puree, sugar, pumpkin pie spice, egg, and vanilla extract.
3. Roll out the pie crusts and cut into small circles.
4. Place a small spoonful of the pumpkin mixture onto each pie crust circle and fold over, sealing the edges.
5. Spray the air fryer basket with cooking spray and place the pie bites in a single layer.
6. Cook for 10 minutes until golden brown.
7. Serve warm.

Nutrition Facts (per serving): Calories: 220 kcal | Protein: 3 g | Carbs: 30 g | Fat: 10 g | Fiber: 2 g | Sugar: 12 g

137. Almond Flour Cookies

Prep time: 10 min | Cook time: 10 min | Servings: 4

Ingredients:

- 1 cup almond flour
- 1/4 cup sugar
- 1/4 cup melted butter

- 1 egg
- 1 teaspoon vanilla extract
- 1/2 teaspoon baking powder
- 1/4 teaspoon salt

Instructions:

1. Preheat air fryer to 180 degrees Celsius.
2. In a large bowl, mix almond flour, sugar, melted butter, egg, vanilla extract, baking powder, and salt until well combined.
3. Drop spoonfuls of dough onto a greased air fryer-safe baking sheet.
4. Cook for 10 minutes, or until golden brown.
5. Let cool slightly before serving.

Nutrition Facts (per serving): Calories: 220 kcal | Protein: 6 g | Carbs: 12 g | Fat: 18 g | Fiber: 3 g | Sugar: 8 g

138. Air Fryer Baked Apples

Prep time: 10 min | Cook time: 15 min | Servings: 4

Ingredients:

- 4 apples, cored
- 1/4 cup brown sugar
- 1/4 cup oats
- 2 tablespoons melted butter
- 1 teaspoon ground cinnamon
- 1/4 teaspoon ground nutmeg
- 1/4 cup chopped nuts (optional)

Instructions:

1. Preheat air fryer to 180 degrees Celsius.
2. In a bowl, mix brown sugar, oats, melted butter, ground cinnamon, ground nutmeg, and chopped nuts if using.
3. Stuff the apples with the mixture.
4. Place the apples in the air fryer basket in a single layer.
5. Cook for 15 minutes until tender and the filling is bubbly.
6. Serve warm.

Nutrition Facts (per serving): Calories: 200 kcal | Protein: 2 g | Carbs: 42 g | Fat: 5 g | Fiber: 6 g | Sugar: 32 g

139. Coconut Macaroons

Prep time: 10 min | Cook time: 10 min | Servings: 4

Ingredients:

- 2 cups shredded coconut
- 1/2 cup sweetened condensed milk
- 1 teaspoon vanilla extract

- 1/4 teaspoon salt

Instructions:

1. Preheat air fryer to 180 degrees Celsius.
2. In a large bowl, mix shredded coconut, sweetened condensed milk, vanilla extract, and salt until well combined.
3. Drop spoonfuls of the mixture onto a greased air fryer-safe baking sheet.
4. Cook for 10 minutes, or until golden brown.
5. Let cool slightly before serving.

Nutrition Facts (per serving): Calories: 250 kcal | Protein: 4 g | Carbs: 32 g | Fat: 12 g | Fiber: 4 g | Sugar: 24 g

140. Air Fryer Cheesecake Bites

Prep time: 15 min | Cook time: 10 min | Servings: 4

Ingredients:

- 1 package cream cheese, softened
- 1/4 cup sugar
- 1 egg
- 1 teaspoon vanilla extract
- 1 package refrigerated pie crusts
- Cooking spray

Instructions:

1. Preheat air fryer to 180 degrees Celsius.
2. In a bowl, mix cream cheese, sugar, egg, and vanilla extract until smooth.
3. Roll out the pie crusts and cut into small circles.
4. Place a small spoonful of the cream cheese mixture onto each pie crust circle and fold over, sealing the edges.
5. Spray the air fryer basket with cooking spray and place the cheesecake bites in a single layer.
6. Cook for 10 minutes until golden brown.
7. Serve warm or chilled.

Nutrition Facts (per serving): Calories: 250 kcal | Protein: 4 g | Carbs: 28 g | Fat: 14 g | Fiber: 1 g | Sugar: 15 g

141. Cinnamon Sugar Donut Holes

Prep time: 10 min | Cook time: 10 min | Servings: 4

Ingredients:

- 1 cup flour
- 1/4 cup sugar
- 1 teaspoon baking powder
- 1/4 teaspoon salt
- 1/2 cup milk
- 1 egg

- 1 teaspoon vanilla extract
- 2 tablespoons melted butter
- 1/4 cup sugar
- 1 teaspoon ground cinnamon

Instructions:

1. Preheat air fryer to 180 degrees Celsius.
2. In a large bowl, mix flour, sugar, baking powder, and salt.
3. Add milk, egg, vanilla extract, and melted butter. Mix until well combined to form a dough.
4. Roll the dough into small balls and place them in the air fryer basket in a single layer.
5. Cook for 10 minutes, shaking the basket halfway through until golden brown.
6. In a separate bowl, mix 1/4 cup sugar and ground cinnamon.
7. While the donut holes are still warm, roll them in the cinnamon sugar mixture. 8. Serve warm.

Nutrition Facts (per serving): Calories: 220 kcal | Protein: 4 g | Carbs: 32 g | Fat: 8 g | Fiber: 1 g | Sugar: 16 g

142. Air Fryer Zucchini Bread

Prep time: 10 min | Cook time: 25 min | Servings: 4

Ingredients:

- 1 cup grated zucchini
- 1 cup flour
- 1/2 cup sugar
- 1/4 cup melted coconut oil
- 1 egg
- 1 teaspoon vanilla extract
- 1/2 teaspoon baking powder
- 1/2 teaspoon baking soda
- 1/2 teaspoon ground cinnamon
- 1/4 teaspoon salt

Instructions:

1. Preheat air fryer to 160 degrees Celsius.
2. In a large bowl, mix grated zucchini, flour, sugar, melted coconut oil, egg, vanilla extract, baking powder, baking soda, ground cinnamon, and salt until well combined.
3. Pour the batter into a greased air fryer-safe baking dish.
4. Cook for 25 minutes, or until a toothpick inserted into the center comes out clean.
5. Let cool slightly before serving.

Nutrition Facts (per serving): Calories: 220 kcal | Protein: 3 g | Carbs: 36 g | Fat: 8 g | Fiber: 2 g | Sugar: 20 g

143. Chocolate-Dipped Strawberries

Prep time: 10 min | Cook time: 5 min | Servings: 4

Ingredients:

- 1 cup dark chocolate chips
- 1 tablespoon coconut oil
- 1 pint fresh strawberries

Instructions:

1. Preheat air fryer to 180 degrees Celsius.
2. In an air fryer-safe bowl, melt the dark chocolate chips and coconut oil, stirring occasionally until smooth.
3. Dip each strawberry into the melted chocolate, allowing the excess to drip off.
4. Place the chocolate-dipped strawberries on a parchment-lined tray.
5. Let the chocolate set at room temperature or refrigerate until firm.
6. Serve chilled.

Nutrition Facts (per serving): Calories: 180 kcal | Protein: 2 g | Carbs: 20 g | Fat: 12 g | Fiber: 4 g | Sugar: 15 g

---

144. Air Fryer Pecan Pie Bars

Prep time: 15 min | Cook time: 20 min | Servings: 4

Ingredients:

- 1 cup flour
- 1/4 cup sugar
- 1/2 cup cold butter, cubed
- 1/2 cup chopped pecans
- 1/4 cup brown sugar
- 1/4 cup corn syrup
- 1 egg
- 1 teaspoon vanilla extract

Instructions:

1. Preheat air fryer to 180 degrees Celsius.
2. In a bowl, mix flour and sugar. Cut in cold butter until crumbly.
3. Press the mixture into an air fryer-safe baking dish.
4. Cook for 10 minutes until golden brown.
5. In a separate bowl, mix chopped pecans, brown sugar, corn syrup, egg, and vanilla extract.
6. Pour the pecan mixture over the baked crust.
7. Cook for an additional 10 minutes until set.
8. Let cool before cutting into bars.
9. Serve at room temperature.

Nutrition Facts (per serving): Calories: 280 kcal | Protein: 3 g | Carbs: 34 g | Fat: 16 g | Fiber: 2 g | Sugar: 20 g

---

145. Lemon Poppy Seed Muffins

Prep time: 10 min | Cook time: 15 min | Servings: 4

Ingredients:

- 1 cup flour
- 1/2 cup sugar
- 1/2 cup milk
- 1/4 cup melted butter
- 1 egg
- 1 tablespoon lemon zest
- 1 tablespoon poppy seeds
- 1 teaspoon baking powder
- 1/2 teaspoon vanilla extract
- 1/4 teaspoon salt

Instructions:

1. Preheat air fryer to 180 degrees Celsius.
2. In a large bowl, mix flour, sugar, baking powder, milk, melted butter, egg, lemon zest, poppy seeds, vanilla extract, and salt until well combined.
3. Pour the batter into greased air fryer-safe muffin cups.
4. Cook for 15 minutes, or until a toothpick inserted into the center comes out clean.
5. Let cool slightly before serving.

Nutrition Facts (per serving): Calories: 220 kcal | Protein: 4 g | Carbs: 32 g | Fat: 8 g | Fiber: 1 g | Sugar: 15 g

146. Air Fryer Carrot Cake

Prep time: 15 min | Cook time: 20 min | Servings: 4

Ingredients:

- 1 cup grated carrots
- 1 cup flour
- 1/2 cup sugar
- 1/4 cup vegetable oil
- 2 eggs
- 1 teaspoon vanilla extract
- 1 teaspoon ground cinnamon
- 1/2 teaspoon baking powder
- 1/2 teaspoon baking soda
- 1/4 teaspoon salt
- 1/4 cup chopped walnuts (optional)

Instructions:

1. Preheat air fryer to 160 degrees Celsius.
2. In a large bowl, mix grated carrots, flour, sugar, vegetable oil, eggs, vanilla extract, ground cinnamon, baking powder, baking soda, salt, and chopped walnuts if using until well combined.
3. Pour the batter into a greased air fryer-safe baking dish.
4. Cook for 20 minutes, or until a toothpick inserted into the center comes out clean.
5. Let cool slightly before serving.

Nutrition Facts (per serving): Calories: 250 kcal | Protein: 4 g | Carbs: 36 g | Fat: 10 g | Fiber: 2 g | Sugar: 20 g

147. Mixed Berry Cobbler

Prep time: 10 min | Cook time: 20 min | Servings: 4

Ingredients:

- 2 cups mixed berries (strawberries, blueberries, raspberries)
- 1/4 cup sugar
- 1 tablespoon lemon juice
- 1/2 cup flour
- 1/4 cup oats
- 1/4 cup brown sugar
- 1/4 cup melted butter
- 1/2 teaspoon ground cinnamon
- 1/4 teaspoon salt

Instructions:

1. Preheat air fryer to 180 degrees Celsius.
2. In a bowl, mix berries, sugar, and lemon juice. Place in an air fryer-safe baking dish.
3. In a separate bowl, mix flour, oats, brown sugar, melted butter, ground cinnamon, and salt until crumbly.
4. Sprinkle the crumble mixture over the berries.
5. Cook for 20 minutes until the topping is golden brown and the berries are bubbly.
6. Serve warm.

Nutrition Facts (per serving): Calories: 250 kcal | Protein: 2 g | Carbs: 40 g | Fat: 10 g | Fiber: 4 g | Sugar: 25 g

148. Air Fryer Chocolate Cake

Prep time: 10 min | Cook time: 20 min | Servings: 4

Ingredients:

- 1 cup flour
- 1/2 cup sugar
- 1/4 cup cocoa powder
- 1/4 cup melted butter
- 2 eggs
- 1 teaspoon vanilla extract
- 1/2 teaspoon baking powder
- 1/4 teaspoon baking soda
- 1/4 teaspoon salt

Instructions:

1. Preheat air fryer to 160 degrees Celsius.

2. In a large bowl, mix flour, sugar, cocoa powder, melted butter, eggs, vanilla extract, baking powder baking soda, and salt until well combined.
3. Pour the batter into a greased air fryer-safe baking dish.
4. Cook for 20 minutes, or until a toothpick inserted into the center comes out clean.
5. Let cool slightly before serving.

Nutrition Facts (per serving): Calories: 250 kcal | Protein: 4 g | Carbs: 36 g | Fat: 10 g | Fiber: 2 g
Sugar: 22 g

149. Peanut Butter Cookies

□□□Prep time: 10 min | Cook time: 10 min | Servings: 4

Ingredients:
- 1 cup peanut butter
- 1/2 cup sugar
- 1 egg
- 1/2 teaspoon vanilla extract
- 1/4 teaspoon baking soda

Instructions:
1. Preheat air fryer to 180 degrees Celsius.
2. In a large bowl, mix peanut butter, sugar, egg, vanilla extract, and baking soda until well combined.
3. Drop spoonfuls of dough onto a greased air fryer-safe baking sheet.
4. Cook for 10 minutes, or until golden brown.
5. Let cool slightly before serving.

Nutrition Facts (per serving): Calories: 250 kcal | Protein: 7 g | Carbs: 20 g | Fat: 16 g | Fiber: 2 g
Sugar: 16 g

150. Air Fryer Fruit Tarts

□□□Prep time: 20 min | Cook time: 10 min | Servings: 4

Ingredients:
- 1 package refrigerated pie crusts
- 1 cup mixed berries
- 1/4 cup sugar
- 1 tablespoon lemon juice
- 1 teaspoon cornstarch
- Cooking spray

Instructions:
1. Preheat air fryer to 180 degrees Celsius.
2. Roll out the pie crusts and cut into small circles to fit in the air fryer basket.
3. In a bowl, mix berries, sugar, lemon juice, and cornstarch.
4. Place a spoonful of the berry mixture onto each pie crust circle.
5. Spray the air fryer basket with cooking spray and place the tarts in a single layer.
6. Cook for 10 minutes until the crust is golden brown and the filling is bubbly.

7. Serve warm.

Nutrition Facts (per serving): Calories: 220 kcal | Protein: 2 g | Carbs: 32 g | Fat: 10 g | Fiber: 3 g | Sugar: 16 g

28 Day - Meal Plan

Day	Breakfast	Lunch	Dinner	Dessert
1	1. Spinach and Feta Egg Muffins	21. Quinoa Stuffed Bell Peppers	71. Lemon Garlic Air Fryer Salmon	131. Air Fryer Apple Chips
2	2. Low-Carb Breakfast Burritos	22. Brown Rice and Veggie Stir-Fry	101. Air Fryer Chicken Breast	127. Crispy Chickpea Salad
3	3. Air Fryer Oatmeal Cups	24. Lentil and Spinach Curry	102. Garlic Herb Pork Chops	50. Air Fryer Zucchini Chips
4	4. Greek Yogurt Parfaits	25. Quinoa and Black Bean Burgers	72. Crispy Air Fryer Shrimp	136. Air Fryer Pumpkin Pie Bites
5	5. Avocado and Egg Toast	27. Air Fryer Falafel	106. BBQ Chicken Thighs	141. Cinnamon Sugar Donut Holes
6	6. Blueberry Almond Breakfast Bars	33. Split Pea Soup	75. Air Fryer Tilapia with Herbs	138. Air Fryer Baked Apples
7	7. Cinnamon Apple Air Fryer Donuts	34. Chickpea and Veggie Buddha Bowl	108. Herb-Crusted Pork Tenderloin	143. Chocolate-Dipped Strawberries
8	8. Veggie-Packed Breakfast Hash	29. Barley and Mushroom Risotto	76. Blackened Salmon	137. Almond Flour Cookies
9	10. Sweet Potato Breakfast Skillet	30. Air Fryer Tofu and Veggie Skewers	103. Air Fryer Meatballs	144. Air Fryer Pecan Pie Bars
10	11. Zucchini and Cheese Frittata	31. Quinoa Salad with Lemon Vinaigrette	96. Air Fryer Sea Bass	33. Air Fryer Granola

11	12. Protein-Packed Pancakes	32. Black Bean Tacos	91. Spicy Tuna Cakes	136. Air Fryer Pumpkin Pie Bites
12	13. Air Fryer French Toast Sticks	35. Air Fryer Bean and Cheese Quesadillas	114. Greek Chicken Skewers	132. Baked Cinnamon Pears
13	14. Mushroom and Spinach Breakfast Quiche	36. Lentil and Veggie Meatballs	90. Air Fryer Halibut Steaks	149. Peanut Butter Cookies
14	15. Chia Seed Pudding	37. Air Fryer Stuffed Zucchini Boats	110. Cajun Chicken Drumsticks	139. Coconut Macaroons
15	16. Air Fryer Breakfast Potatoes	39. Three-Bean Salad	93. Honey Mustard Salmon	140. Air Fryer Cheesecake Bites
16	17. Healthy Breakfast Sandwich	40. Chickpea and Avocado Salad	86. Lemon Pepper Air Fryer Trout	148. Air Fryer Chocolate Cake
17	18. Egg and Veggie Breakfast Cups	41. Air Fryer Veggie Samosas	115. BBQ Ribs	145. Lemon Poppy Seed Muffins
18	19. Air Fryer Granola	42. Black Bean and Corn Salsa	100. Air Fryer Swordfish	147. Mixed Berry Cobbler
19	20. Banana Nut Muffins	43. Quinoa and Veggie Stir-Fry	120. Air Fryer Chicken Parmesan	45. Air Fryer Edamame
20	21. Quinoa Stuffed Bell Peppers	44. Red Lentil Dhal	118. Spicy Italian Sausage	150. Air Fryer Fruit Tarts
21	12. Protein-Packed Pancakes	26. Brown Rice Pilaf	123. Herb-Marinated Lamb Chops	142. Air Fryer Zucchini Bread

22	4. Greek Yogurt Parfaits	27. Air Fryer Falafel	112. Teriyaki Chicken	131. Air Fryer Apple Chips
23	10. Sweet Potato Breakfast Skillet	29. Barley and Mushroom Risotto	105. Air Fryer Beef Kabobs	141. Cinnamon Sugar Donut Holes
24	6. Blueberry Almond Breakfast Bars	25. Quinoa and Black Bean Burgers	74. Garlic Butter Shrimp Skewers	133. Chocolate Avocado Brownies
25	5. Avocado and Egg Toast	34. Chickpea and Veggie Buddha Bowl	78. Honey Glazed Salmon	138. Air Fryer Baked Apples
26	14. Mushroom and Spinach Breakfast Quiche	36. Lentil and Veggie Meatballs	122. BBQ Chicken Wings	144. Air Fryer Pecan Pie Bars
27	13. Air Fryer French Toast Sticks	33. Split Pea Soup	77. Air Fryer Crab Cakes	137. Almond Flour Cookies
28	15. Chia Seed Pudding	37. Air Fryer Stuffed Zucchini Boats	71. Lemon Garlic Air Fryer Salmon	140. Air Fryer Cheesecake Bites

Bonus:
- Extra Video Recipes with step-by-step explanations!

27729204R00060